COLLECTING POT LIDS

Edward Fletcher

COLLECTING POT LIDS

Pitman Publishing

First published 1975

Sir Isaac Pitman and Sons Ltd
Pitman House, Parker Street, Kingsway, London WC2B 5PB
PO Box 46038, Banda Street, Nairobi, Kenya

Pitman Publishing Pty Ltd
Pitman House, 158 Bouverie Street, Carlton, Victoria 3053, Australia

Pitman Publishing Corporation
6 East 43rd Street, New York, NY 10017, USA

The Copp Clark Publishing Company
517 Wellington Street West, Toronto 135, Canada

© Edward Fletcher 1975

ISBN 0 273 00818 8

Printed in Belgium by Les Presses Saint-Augustin, Bruges - DF 8224

G. 46: 13

Contents

Acknowledgements

Whenever I write a book nowadays I find myself indebted to more and more people for help, advice, and encouragement. This present volume is no exception and I wish to express my gratitude to the following:

Gregory Payne, National Secretary of the British Bottle Collectors' Club. Without his help as researcher, photographer, and motor mechanic, the project might have been abandoned.

Mr A. Wright, Editor of *The Chemist and Druggist*, who kindly allowed me to photograph advertisements from the *Chemist's and Druggist's Diary* and gave permission for their reproduction here. I am also grateful to Mr Wright for the temporary use of his office as a photographic studio.

Miss Jones and Miss Church of the Pharmaceutical Society's Library for their help in finding research material.

June Heath of Iver, one of Britain's most enthusiastic black and white pot lid collectors and a faithful friend. Also her mother for many welcome cups of tea.

David Lewis of Harrogate, who supplied some of the photographs and accompanied me on an exciting dig.

All other members of the British Bottle Collectors' Club for their active interest in dump-digging and their loyalty as my readers.

And Edwina Conner, my unpaid literary agent.

Introduction

On the outskirts of every town in Britain – and many of those countries which were part of the British Empire or which imported large quantities of British goods during the late Victorian and Edwardian eras – lie forgotten sites used in those days for the disposal of household refuse. Dig into one of them and you will unearth an assortment of beautiful glass and ceramic containers and other objects which provide intimate details of the everyday lives of those generations immediately preceding our own.

This fascinating pastime has captured the imagination of many people in recent years. Dump-digging has become a major leisure activity in Britain, the United States, Canada, Australia, New Zealand, South Africa, and several other countries. In the homes of those who spend their weekends digging collectors' items out of the ground you will find bottles and jars once used in grandmother's kitchen; flagons and flasks in which grandfather bought his favourite tipple; pots and phials used by quack doctors and chemists to dispense their amazing cures; even toys of china and glass which children played with a hundred years ago when plastics had not been invented.

You will also find pot lids – glazed earthenware covers for small pots which once held toothpaste, fish paste, face cream, hair preparations and other commodities unsuitable for packaging in bottles. Some have beautiful coloured pictures of stately homes, famous people, or well-known scenes printed on them; others carry only the name of the chemist or grocer who sold the pot together with a brief description of the contents printed in black lettering against the white earthenware of the lid. Coloured or black and white, these pot lids are highly prized by all dump-diggers and most likely to take pride of place in any collection of historical containers.

The literature of dump-digging already includes several books and magazines devoted to bottles and other dump finds; but the few books available on pot lids are little more than catalogues of coloured varieties. Although of interest to the coloured lid collector who buys from antique shops, they give no practical advice to the reader who wishes to form a collection by digging his lids out of the ground. What is even more frustrating to those who already enjoy rubbish dump exploration is that available literature either dismisses black and white lids in a few paragraphs, or suggests they are of secondary importance to pot lid collectors.

This may well be the case for the collector who seeks his lids in high-class antique shops, but it is far from true for the dump-digger who might find fifty black and white lids before he encounters a coloured specimen. There are around five hundred known coloured lids; there are probably as many as four thousand different black and whites. Furthermore, there are at least 30,000 dump-diggers in Britain alone who have collections of black and white lids ranging from half a dozen specimens to display cabinets holding two or three hundred. Similar figures can be quoted for Australia and New Zealand, while the total number of black and white pot lid collectors in the rest of the world probably equals Britain's figure.

The importance of any group of objects as collectors' items must surely be measured by the number of collectors who take an interest in them. By this yardstick black and white lids are clearly of considerable significance, and we can infer from this premise that a book which treats black and white lids with the reverence they deserve is long overdue. Of course, coloured pot lid collecting has a much longer history; it was popular at a time when black and white lids were regarded as fit only for relegation to the household dustbin. But it must be noted that coloured lids were intended to become collectors' items when they were first produced. Those manufacturers of fish pastes, cosmetics, and other commodities who went to the expense of packaging their wares in pots with coloured lids were motivated by the same desire to increase sales that now encourages cornflake manufacturers to mix plastic aeroplanes with our breakfast cereal. They were more subtle in their attempts to increase sales. Instead of giving away a worthless piece of plastic backed by massive advertising to persuade the public that it was, in fact, highly desirable, they offered an object of beauty which required much skill in manufacture, and they relied on the public's appreciation of beauty and craftmanship to ensure that the pots and their contents sold well. It was a sales policy successful for more than forty years, until the costs of producing the containers became prohibitive. By that time coloured lid collecting was established and it has continued to attract newcomers to the world of antiques ever since.

Why then are there now far more collectors of black and white lids when coloured lids had such a flying start? The answer to this question lies partly in the current prices of coloured lids, which have soared in recent years because the number of coloured lids coming on the market has failed to keep pace with demand. A new collector must consider himself fortunate if he can buy one of the commonest coloured lids at £25, while rare varieties will change hands at £1,000 or more. Such expenditure on a hobby is out of the question for the man in the street, who must remain in the street with his nose pressed up against the window pane of the antique shop – or find a substitute for the coloured lids he cannot afford. Fortunately, the recent popularity of dump-digging has brought to light thousands of black and white lids which our grandparents and great-grandparents threw into their dustbins. Commercial diggers have encountered enormous demand for these lids from non-digging collectors, while those who dig to add to their own collections have seen the value of their humble lids rise within a few years from less than £1 each to £5, £10, even £25 for rarities. Thus, a shortage of the coloured lids, which first introduced the hobby to a small section of the public, has helped to create widespread interest in the black and whites once regarded as uncollectable.

However, short supply of coloured lids is not the sole reason for the current popularity of black and whites. Large-scale Victorian dump excavations which have brought so many fascinating objects to light in recent years have also created much interest in the history of Victorian containers. Most dump-diggers soon progress from an acquisitive urge to dig up as many objects as they can from a site to a thirsting desire to know as much as possible about their finds. The questions which interest them above all others are: who used a particular bottle, jar, or pot, and what did it contain? Only very rarely do coloured lids include in their decorations any information about the contents of their pots or the names of those who sold them. Black and whites, on the other hand, provide a wealth of information within their transfers: names and addresses of suppliers; details of contents; the purposes for which contents were used; even the prices at which many pots sold – all indelibly recorded on objects measuring less than four inches in diameter. Thus a single black and white lid might tell the student of Victorian container history that Mrs Hummerstone's Celebrated Heal-All Ointment was made and put into pots by Mrs Ellen Hale who once traded at Brandon Street, Walworth, and who later removed to 26 York Street, London. Thrown in for good measure on this particular lid, the student will find a head and shoulders portrait of Mrs Hummerstone and the information that Mrs Hale also made oils for rheumatism and bronchitis. Another find might reveal that Mr F. Perkins of Harrogate, proprietor of the Harrogate Wood Violet, prepared and sold in oblong pots a 'cherry areca nut tooth paste' which was an elegant preparation for whitening the teeth without injuring the enamel, and which was invaluable to smokers and for rendering the breath sweet and fragrant.

This is Victorian advertising at its naive best; it is also invaluable information for the digger who wishes to date other objects he finds in association with his pot lids. Many an unembossed and unidentifiable bottle has been dated by the transfer on a black and white lid found nearby. The lid may be neither so beautiful nor so valuable as a coloured specimen but it is, nevertheless, a find which any digger will be delighted to add to his collection. Unlike paper labels which quickly deteriorate, the transfers on pot lids survive long periods of burial in the ground; and because black and white transfers provide the student of container history with such valuable information, these lids have become his most important finds.

This book is addressed primarily to the reader who wishes to dig his collection of pot lids out of the ground. It explains how information on those sites which hold large numbers of pot lids is obtained; how that information is used to pinpoint site locations; and how the sites are correctly and most profitably excavated. Any newcomer to Victorian and Edwardian dump-digging who applies the rules it sets out will certainly find pot lids – both coloured and black and white – and experience the pleasures and satisfactions of do-it-yourself antique hunting already enjoyed by diggers everywhere. Established pot lid collectors will also find plenty to interest them within these pages whether or not they take an active interest in digging. Much of the information contained in the historical notes is gathered together for the first time. It has been gleaned from newspaper advertisements, from the catalogues of wholesale chemists, from the records of the British Bottle Collectors' Club, and from many other sources which contain references to pot lids. The notes on black and white lids are undoubtedly the most comprehensive yet published and they will prove invaluable to the collector who wishes to know as much as possible about pot lid history.

Almost all black and white lids and many coloured specimens find their way into collections after being dug out of the ground. They survive their long burial extremely well, but inevitably some are found which have been damaged by the rough treatment received in their journeys from household dustbins to the dumps. Restoring these lids to collectable condition is an important aspect of the hobby and one which is fully covered here in the chapter on cleaning and repairs. The non-digging collector who wishes to acquire lids at minimum expense will find this chapter especially useful. If he masters the simple techniques used to repair damaged lids he will be able to buy specimens with minor cracks, chips and other imperfections very cheaply from diggers. When restored they will provide him with an excellent collection for a very modest outlay.

No book on pot lid collecting would be complete without some photographs of the lids themselves. The examples shown in the illustrated section at the end of this book are included to give newcomers to the hobby some idea of the wide variety which can be found by dump-diggers. The collector who already owns a number of lids will find the price guide which the book also contains even more useful. It lists and values all black and white lids in the collections of members of the British Bottle Collectors' Club who combined their information on known black and white lids in order to make the list as comprehensive as possible. Because there are thousands of Victorian and Edwardian dumps throughout Britain yet to be explored, which certainly hold many black and white lids at present unknown to diggers and collectors, the list is incomplete. If this book encourages diggers to add to it by finding those unexplored dumps the task of writing the book will have been worth while.

1 Historical notes

Hand-painted pots

Long before transfer-printed pot lids first appeared at the beginning of the nineteenth century pots for ointments, pills, dentifrices and other products were being manufactured by many potteries throughout Britain. They were blue and white vessels of tin-enamelled earthenware, called 'patch boxes' by the potters who made them, and used by druggists, dentists, bear's grease packers, and shopkeepers, who probably bought no more than two or three hundred each in a single year. Two standard shapes were made – straight-sided round pots and pedestal-shaped pots – and each pottery would make large batches decorated with uniform blue rings or stripes to be sold, by the gross, to retailers who added their own paper labels to indicate the pot's contents when filled.

By 1750 a few retailers whose yearly sales of potted products justified the expense were having their pots 'customized' by the potters who would add hand-lettered traders' names. The practice grew as sales methods became more sophisticated, and a few years later pots bearing traders' names, addresses and, occasionally, brief descriptions of the pot's contents were being hand-lettered by several potteries. One of the earliest surviving examples is a bear's grease pot dating from the late 1750s now in the Fitzwilliam Museum, Cambridge. It carries the inscription, 'prepared by T. Townshend and sold only by C. King, Chymist, Hay Market' together with a handpainted picture of a bear.

On-the-glaze printing

Pots which had to be decorated entirely by hand were, of course, quite unsuitable for the age of mass production and nationally known branded goods which was just around the corner. The necessity for speed in decoration required for quantity production encouraged potters to experiment with new ideas for embellishing all types of pottery. Among the first to achieve success at rapid printing of single-colour designs on pottery were two gentlemen from Liverpool named Sadler and Green who claimed in a patent dated 1756 that they did 'within the space of six hours... print upwards of twelve hundred tiles of different patterns'. Soon large quantities of undecorated plates, cups, jugs and other tablewares were being despatched from potteries in Staffordshire – including that of Josiah Wedgwood – to the workshops of Messrs Sadler and Green in Liverpool for decoration by the new process.

The method used involved printing the design on top of the existing glaze in a special ink which was hardened by re-firing the pottery again at a low temperature. The design produced in this way was, of course, subject to wear; but by the beginning of the nineteenth century many potteries had discovered the secret of *underglaze* printing in one colour – black, blue, brown, pink or green – which produced a permanent design beneath the surface of the pot.

Underglaze transfer printing

Underglaze transfer printing was carried out in the following way.

A copper plate was first engraved with the required design and ink applied to it with a soft piece of leather. Strips of specially prepared paper were then pressed on to the copper plate to obtain impressions of the designs and these paper prints were *transferred* to the surfaces of the pots to be decorated at the unglazed or biscuit stage of manufacture. When the paper was peeled from the surface the ink remained and the pots could be despatched to a hardening kiln where oils in the ink were burned out to leave behind the metallic oxide. Glaze was now applied and the pots re-fired until the glaze fused with the ink and the transfers became integral parts of the finished pots. In this way a uniform design could be repeated many times in a single day. The age of mass-produced underglaze decorated pottery had arrived.

Mass production

In the first quarter of the nineteenth century Britain was transformed from 'a nation of shopkeepers' to a nation of manufacturers, wholesalers and shopkeepers. The days of the local chemist and grocer who made up packets with brown paper and string and who potted their secret remedies, ointments and pills in hand-painted blue and white striped delftware with hand-printed paper labels began to draw to a close. A new era of machine-made products and nationwide distribution dawned; with it came the need for more attractive, more sales-stimulating containers for the thousands of exciting products being made by Britain's new manufacturers. The principle of lithography had recently been discovered, and machines that could make cardboard boxes had just been invented. A new industry, packaging, was about to emerge. Those potteries which had previously supplied hand-decorated pots and jars by the gross to family chemists and provisions merchants now eagerly sought larger orders for transfer-printed wares from the fast-growing manufacturing chemists and wholesalers beginning to market

Burgoyne, Burbidges & Co.

JOHNSON STREET WAREHOUSES

Typical warehouse of a busy wholesale chemist in the early nineteenth century.

their own branded goods through national networks of retail outlets. Several potteries developed new methods of making earthenware pots which, in the eighteenth century, had been formed on traditional potter's wheels. Now moulds were employed to speed up the process and to ensure the production of pots of uniform size.

One pottery highly successful in capturing substantial orders for druggists' sundries was the firm of F. & R. Pratt of Fenton, Staffordshire. The company was soon supplying large quantities of transfer-printed earthenware to manufacturing and wholesale chemists throughout Britain. Dispensing pots, jars, hot water bottles, babies' feeding bottles and many similar products made today in glass, plastics and other materials were in those days manufactured in ceramics. In use they came into contact with hot water and oily substances which would have quickly removed paper labels; underglaze transfer-printing was, therefore, the ideal method of decorating them with trade marks, brand names, instructions for use and other embellishments. Pratt's engravers, together with those of many other potteries, were kept busy with new work as more and more companies sprang up, each requiring ornate trade marks and designs. The Fenton pottery quickly established a reputation for the excellence of its engravings and the quality of the transfer-printed wares it turned out.

Coloured pot lids

At first potters were limited to the use of black or a single colour when decorating their wares; but it was a logical step from printing in one colour to the production of multi-coloured

3

Underglaze transfer-printed labels were used on a variety of chemists' sundries, including the inhalers shown here.

transfers. Manufacturers were constantly experimenting to find suitable inks, glazes and methods of printing in exact registration. A wide colour range of inks that burned out at the same temperature had to be found; glazes that did not vitrify too soon or too late were required; and a means of transferring each colour from engraving to paper to pottery without mis-alignment had to be invented.

Early successes at adding colour to transfer-printed ware were achieved by using a contrasting background. Solid colour and opaque inks were used, so exact registration between the ground colour and the picture or lettering superimposed was not required. Another method used was to print a monochrome picture on the surface of the pot and then to add several more colours by hand before the glaze was applied. By the late 1830 multi-colour printing on paper had been perfected; by the 1840

F. & R. Pratt, and probably two or three other potteries, had overcome the problems of transfer printing subjects in two or more colours on pottery and had discovered the secret of perfect balance between the firing temperatures of glazes and inks to bring the latter to their full colour. It was now possible to produce underglaze multi-coloured pictures and designs on pottery without hand-painting.

F. & R. Pratt were already supplying transfer-printed pots with lids in monochrome and with coloured backgrounds to their customers in the chemist and druggist trades. Some of those customers, notably those selling more expensive products to the upper-class markets, soon became interested in the new transfers for which the pottery was rapidly becoming famous and it was at some time in the late 1840s that the first multi-coloured Pratt pot lids were made.

Bear's grease, a very expensive product by this time, was one of the first commodities to be packaged in pots with coloured lids. As a hair dressing its use dates back far beyond the first underglaze transfer-printed pottery; live bears were being imported from Russia to meet demand from balding members of the upper classes before 1700 and the business had been invigorated by a plentiful supply of bears from North America as trans-Atlantic shipping trade began to boom in the eighteenth century. An advertisement from the *Public Advertiser* dated 4 January 1765 is typical of many:

'A young fat bear is killed, and is to be seen at R. Sangwine's, Perfumer, at the Sign of the Rose, No. 36, in the Strand, where any Lady or Gentleman may see the fat cut off the bear's back at two shillings an ounce. After three days it will be melted down and put into pots for sale at the above price.

This lid, made in the 1840s, was printed in blue, black and green. The green ink was applied by hand before glazing. It is one of the earliest coloured pot lids and was probably made by T. J. & J. Mayer.

5

It is best to use honey water with it which may be had at the same place.'

Another advertiser pointed out to prospective customers that his bear had 'been fed on bread for three years past, by which means the fat is uncommonly fine'; while many others invited customers to witness the actual killing as proof that the potted hair dressing was indeed genuine bear's grease. This gruesome spectacle could no longer be seen in Britain by the 1840s; the grease was by this time being imported in bulk from abroad and packaged by wholesalers. Nor was the killing or any aspect of the actual manufacturing process considered a suitable subject with which to illustrate the lids of bear's grease pots. Some of the early black and white examples showed a chained bear, and one or two of the coloured lids produced by a combination of printing and hand-painting depicted bears in the wild; but on the majority of multi-coloured lids the animals were endowed with human characteristics: bears dressed in human clothing; young bears attending school and being taught to read by an old grizzly wearing a mortar-board; and one example with the inscription, 'Alas, poor bruin!' which shows an unhappy bear being teased by young boys throwing snowballs. Such sentimentality helped, no doubt, to sell the product.

A multi-coloured picture showing the slaughter of a noble bear probably would not have boosted sales of bear's grease;

Early black and white lids from bear's grease pots. Atkinson retained the chained bear design on his lids for more than half a century.

but a delightful scene showing shrimpers at work with their nets did much to encourage sales of shrimp paste. This illustration was one of several commissions received by F. & R. Pratt and other makers of coloured lids from the shrimp-paste manufacturers of Pegwell Bay near Ramsgate who, like the bear's grease packers, were quick to appreciate the sales potential of a highly coloured pot. They sold most of their produce in the newly popular resorts along the south coast which had recently become accessible to thousands of visitors with the advent of the railways. A pot of shrimp paste with a pretty coloured lid was just the thing for beach picnics or for taking home as a souvenir of a stay at the seaside. One of the leading manufacturers in Pegwell Bay was a gentleman named Sam Banger who had a series of coloured lids made showing views of the village of Pegwell Bay and the surrounding coastline. On some of the lids the engraver included Sam Banger's factory, complete with signboard in the picture, a novel way of adding one's trading name and address to a package.

Other companies, including such up-and-coming firms as Cadbury Bros, J. S. Fry, and John Burgess & Son, were soon customers of F. & R. Pratt. They were happy to allow the entire lids of many of the pots they ordered to be given over to 'art for art's sake'. Company names and descriptions of the pot's contents were relegated to the pot itself so that the engraver could use the complete area of the lid for his picture.

This might have been a stately home, a view of a well-known city or town, a portrait of a famous person, or a picture of animals, birds or fishes. The pot's contents might have been chocolate sauce, meat paste, anchovies, or any one of a dozen delicacies and toilet articles being offered to an increasingly affluent public in these attractive packages.

At the Great Exhibition of 1851, F. & R. Pratt received special mention by the Jury for their underglaze multi-coloured printing. Much of the credit for the outstanding quality of their work must go to their chief engraver, Jesse Austin, who was employed by the pottery for more than thirty years until his death in 1879. During this period he made hundreds of engravings for Pratt's transfer-printed wares, and many of these were used on the company's pot lids.

Although the largest producers of coloured lids, F. & R. Pratt did not have a monopoly of the market. There were a number of competitors, one of the most successful in the early days being T. J. & J. Mayer of the Dale Hall Pottery, Longport, Staffordshire, who, like Pratt, displayed coloured lids at the Great Exhibition. According to the Exhibition catalogue Mayer's stand included coloured lids for meat-paste pots. These were probably made for Crosse & Blackwell, one of Mayer's first customers. After 1855 the Dale Hall Pottery was owned by a series of partnerships including Mayer & Elliot, Bates, Walker & Co., and several others. The last owner, James Gildea, was making wares for chemists and druggists as late as 1888 and it is almost certain that coloured pot lids were made intermittently at Dale Hall throughout their period of popularity. Lids which can definitely be attributed to the pottery include one showing the Bear Pit in Regent's Park and another showing a view of the Houses of Parliament. Pegwell Bay was also featured on Dale Hall lids, an indication that, like F. & R. Pratt, they got some of their business from the shrimping trade.

Coloured pot lids were expensive to manufacture. Even at the height of their popularity in the 1860s they were only used by a few hundred companies able to absorb their cost in the price of the luxury items the pots contained. This marriage of art and sales promotion which transformed a functional container to a work of beauty was only possible because there were customers prepared to pay a few shillings for a pot of fish paste with a coloured lid when pots of equally nourishing fish paste with black and white lids could be had for sixpence. True, a few of those customers kept the empty pots and became the first pot lid collectors; but others simply threw them into the dustbin after the contents had been used. For this extravagance today's collectors are most grateful!

Eventually, the combined effects of rising production costs, competition from other packaging materials, and changing fashions put an end to coloured pot lids. Bear's grease went out of use; anchovy paste sold even better in a clear glass jar; and a multi-coloured tin or cardboard box could be bought for a fraction of the price of a coloured earthenware pot. It also weighed much less – a great advantage at a time when ever-increasing amounts of merchandise were being transported by road, rail and sea to markets at home and abroad. By 1890 production of coloured lids was down to a trickle, and shortly after the beginning of the twentieth century it had ceased altogether – save for a few specimens of inferior workmanship that failed to match the Victorian skills, and occasional commemorative issues of originals to satisfy demand from modern collectors.

The black and white pot lid market
There are three equally important reasons why pots with black and white transfer-printed lids continued to be used as commercial packages long after coloured lids had fallen out of general use. Firstly, they cost far less to make and could, therefore, be purchased and used by many companies unable to afford the luxury of packaging their products in pots with coloured lids. This large market enabled the potteries that made them to withstand competition from other forms of packaging far longer than was possible with coloured lids for which the market was small and which felt the effects of reduced demand very quickly.

Secondly, many of the products which were sold in earthenware pots in the nineteenth century, notably toothpastes, cold creams, and other toilet articles, could not be packaged in

Opposite :
Standardized transfers like these could be sold to many chemists, making it economical for potteries to turn out large numbers of transfer-printed pots for sale in small lots to individual shopkeepers.

Boots was one of the first companies to open a string of retail shops selling branded goods made in the company's own factory. Many of the products were sold in transfer-printed pots.

9

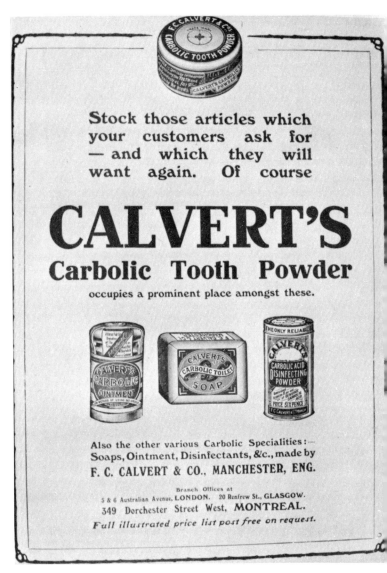

Typical of the advertising aimed at promoting sales of branded goods which became widespread after 1880.

card-board and were considered unsuitable for packaging in glass. (Even today one does not see these products in clear glass containers.) Paper labels, however inexpensive printers made them, were quite useless on pots containing greasy creams and those which came into contact with water as often as toothpaste pots. The only secure label was an underglaze transfer, (or 'burnt-in' label as they were sometimes called) and because most toothpastes and cold creams sold quite cheaply, the only choice for the majority of vendors was a black and white transfer. (Of the several hundred toothpaste pot lids recovered in recent years by dump-diggers less than half a dozen were coloured lids.

The third reason for the widespread and long-lasting use of black and white pot lids is the most interesting; to explain it we must go back to the very beginnings of transfer-printed pot lid history. When potteries began making them in the early

S. Maw, Son & Thompson sold a range of branded goods in transfer-printed pots, including their Ambrosial Shaving Cream. The company changed its name to S. Maw, Son, & Sons in the 1880s.

years of the nineteenth century they faced the same problem that had confronted delftware pot makers a century before – there was a shortage of customers able to place large enough orders to justify the expense of making an engraving. To overcome this the potters turned out standardized pots with black and white lids bearing the words, 'Bear's Grease', 'Toothpaste' or 'Cold Cream'. These pots were then sold in small lots to different customers as the earlier delftware pots had been; but this was not a happy state of affairs for the small shopkeeper who still had to attach a name and address label to the base of the pot if he was to gain any advertising benefit from the new containers.

The necessity to sell a sufficient number of transfer-printed pots to cover the initial cost of the engraving must also have been a constant problem to those potteries making coloured lids. True, many of their customers were large companies able to place substantial orders, but as production costs increased the problem must have become more acute. It might account for the large number of coloured lids which carry no lettering; several lettered pot bases made for different customers could have been produced to match the same lid.

In the black and white market another solution came with the growth of large manufacturing and wholesale chemists. These companies were soon ordering thousands of lids a year embellished with their own company and brand names. Many

HOLLOWAY'S
PILLS & OINTMENT
ARE MEDICINES OF MARVELLOUS EFFICACY,
AND
TWO SAFE RECOMMENDATIONS.

HOLLOWAY'S PILLS

Assure against serious illness by thoroughly cleansing the system of all impurities and toning it up to the point of resistance. They produce functional activity and regularity, and are the surest remedy for Indigestion, Bilious Attacks, Feverishness, Headache, Dizziness and Depression. They give renewed vitality, and are invaluable to Females.

HOLLOWAY'S OINTMENT

Assures against Aches and Pains, Rheumatism, Sciatica, Lumbago, Stiffness of the Limbs and Joints, Sprains and Strains. It cures Bad Legs, Old Wounds and Sores with amazing rapidity, and is magical in the treatment of all Skin affections. In cases of Asthma, Bronchitis, Sore Throat, Hoarseness and Tightness of the Chest it gives immediate and lasting relief.

Counter Bills, Billheads, &c., with Retailer's Name, FREE, also Mutual Bills for House to House distribution—Specimens and Terms on application to

THOMAS HOLLOWAY, 113 Southwark Street, LATE 78 NEW OXFORD STREET, **LONDON.**

small chemists' shopowners were persuaded by attractive profit margins to abandon sales of their own products and to stock the branded goods in their place. These sales campaigns were backed by large-scale advertising from the manufacturers and wholesalers. Phrases such as 'sold by all reputable chemists in London' and 'may be had from chemists throughout the Kingdom' began to appear in daily newspapers. In the early days

Holloway's ointment was one of many 'cure-alls' popular in the late nineteenth century. Today the lid of the pot is equally popular with collectors.

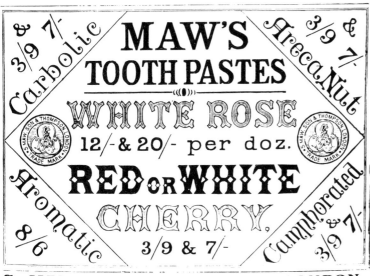

MAW'S TOOTH PASTES

Carbolic 3/9 & 7/-

AreaNut 3/9 & 7/-

WHITE ROSE
12/- & 20/- per doz.
RED or WHITE
CHERRY,
3/9 & 7/-

Aromatic 8/6

Camphorated 3/9 & 7/-

S. MAW, SON & THOMPSON, LONDON.

Numerous brands of toothpaste were offered for sale, and there was no shortage of choice in toothbrushes.

THE NEW PATENT

TOOTH BRUSH.

Dr. Horsey's Oriental Fibre Tooth Brush.

Take short up and down stroke, holding handle down.

DIRECTIONS

USE WATER FREELY.

Squeeze brush head after using, like a sponge.

The Brush is made of solid wood from a tree grown in Arabia; it has been in use by the natives as early as B.C. 3000. It contains properties most beneficial to the teeth and gums. It is a perfect Cleanser—the inside as well as the outside surface can be easily reached, a thing most impossible by an ordinary brush.

In Boxes containing
12 refills, **1/-**
Handles,
Imperishable, **1/-**

MANUFACTORY

Al Arak Works, FARNHAM, SURREY.

OF ALL WHOLESALE HOUSES.

13

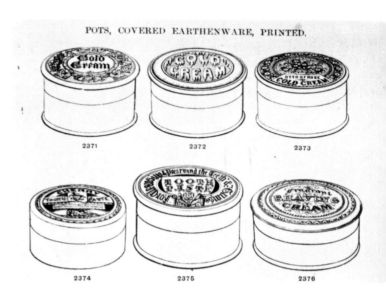

POTS, COVERED EARTHENWARE, PRINTED.

Illustration from a wholesale chemist's catalogue of the 1890s, showing a range of attractive 'off the shelf' transfer-printed pots.

of the industry these announcements were tucked away in the personal columns; but as the power of advertising was realized and competition between manufacturers and wholesalers increased, the advertisements grew to include illustrations of the products and brand names in larger and more eye-catching letters.

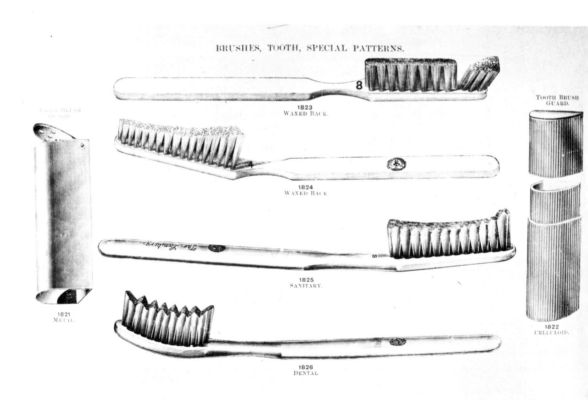

BRUSHES, TOOTH, SPECIAL PATTERNS.

Sales of lids after 1880

By the 1880s, when the use of coloured pot lids began to decline, chemists' shops were doing a roaring trade as public interest in health and hygiene grew. Quack medicines, pills, ointments, perfumed soaps, cosmetics, and, most of all, toothpastes were selling in enormous quantities. As many of these products were sold in earthenware pots with 'burnt-in' labels, the potteries making them were delighted and more anxious than ever to increase their share of the market. Wholesale chemists were equally aware of the opportunities for increased sales, and the two industries now cooperated to boost sales of factory-made toothpastes, cold creams and other products in transfer-printed pots.

Despite earlier attempts by the wholesalers to discourage the practice, there were still thousands of chemists who preferred to make up their own pastes and creams and to package them in plain pots with paper labels rather than sell the products made and packed by wholesalers. In renewed attempts to end this competition wholesale chemists became wholesalers of transfer-printed pots. They placed large orders with the potteries for a variety of toothpaste and cold cream pots with newly designed and more attractive transfers. These were then offered to retail chemists at low prices, together with free paper bands printed with the retailer's name and address. The paper bands were wrapped around the base of the pot after it was filled to keep the lid in place, thus leaving the attractive transfer visible to the customer.

By the 1890s the smallest retailer was able to buy transfer-printed pots with his own name and address 'burnt in' – thanks to competition for his business between wholesale chemists.

A NEW DEPARTURE.

COVERED POTS UP TO DATE

Up to the present it has been almost impossible to get anything really original and artistic in the designs submitted for Covered Pots for Tooth Paste, Cold Cream, &c., &c., and there has been what is usually known as a "long-felt want" for something more in keeping with the present School of Elegant Pharmacy. We have, therefore, organised a staff of skilled artists for originating and improving special designs to suit the varied requirements of our Customers, and are in a position to give perfect satisfaction in the execution of any orders entrusted to us.

Ayrton & Saunders

SQUARE CROYDEN POTS.

White or Cream Coloured Earthenware.

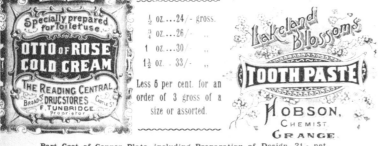

½ oz....24/- gross.
¾ oz....26/- ,,
1 oz....30/- ,,
1½ oz. . 33/- ,,

Less 6 per cent. for an order of 3 gross of a size or assorted.

Part Cost of Copper Plate, including Preparation of Design, 21 - net.

We also supply Round and Octagon Pots of all sizes and styles, and shall be pleased to supply Illustrated Sheets of Stock Designs on application.

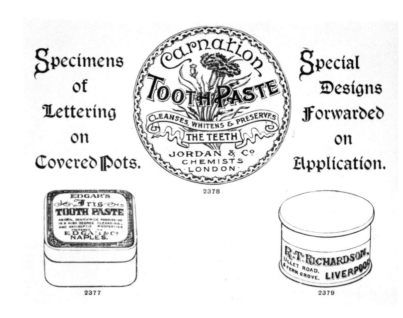

There was, of course, a great deal of prestige in having one's name and address 'burnt-in' on the lids of the pots sold on one's premises. Larger retailers with perhaps half a dozen shops in as many towns were able to do this because they could place big orders with the potteries; but the small retailer with only one shop had to be content to see his name and address on a paper band. However, the potteries and the wholesalers eventually managed to overcome even this thorny problem. Engravers designed lids which had ornate borders and attractive lettering to describe the pot's contents, and which also had a space within the complete design left blank. A second transfer carrying the retailer's name and address could be neatly fitted into this space to provide a complete 'burnt-in' label for any customer. When a space could not be made within the transfer on the lid the retailer's name and address was transfer-printed on the body of the pot.

The final step in the capitulation of small retailers to big business came when they were at last persuaded to hand over secret recipes for their own creams and pastes so that these could be made up at the factory and packaged in the retailer's own pots which were, of course, already stacked on the factory's shelves. For the retailer this meant no more mixing and measuring in the back of the shop, no more licking and sticking of paper labels, no more loss of prestige because one did not have 'burnt-in' pot lids. For big business, of course, it meant totally dependent retail outlets.

Pot lids overseas
Overseas markets also helped to boost sales of lids. F. & R. Pratt received at least one commission from an American perfume manufacturer for a specially designed coloured lid, but

H. GILBERTSON & SONS.

BEST AND CHEAPEST DRUGGISTS' SUNDRIES FOR ALL MARKETS.
SEE PRICE LIST.

CHERRY · TOOTH · PASTE
FOR CLEANSING & PRESERVING THE TEETH & GUMS.
MANUFACTURED BY H. GILBERTSON & SONS LONDON

ENGLISH MANUFACTURE.

ENGLISH MANUFACTURE.

...ds bearing our TRADE MARK are unequalled in quality at prices charged. Illustrated Price List sent free on application

11 ST. ANDREW STREET, HOLBORN CIRCUS, LONDON.
Telegraphic Address " FRANGIPANE LONDON "

substantial export market in colour-printed pots was never established. Pots with black and white transfer-printed lids were, however, shipped in large quantities to the United States and to all parts of the British Empire. The commonest pot lid found in nineteenth-century American dumps today is one used for Jewsbury & Brown's Oriental Toothpaste. These export lids have the word 'England' added beneath the company's address which was in Manchester.

Another lid which found its way into rubbish dumps in many countries was that of John Gosnell's Cherry Toothpaste. In a late nineteenth century advertisement the company quoted from a globe-trotter's diary': 'I have found John Gosnell & Co.'s Cherry Toothpaste in all parts of the world. It appears

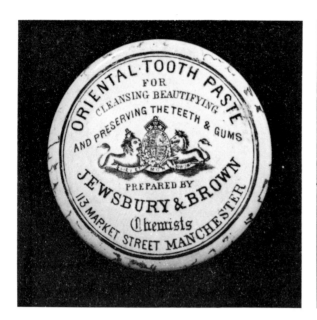
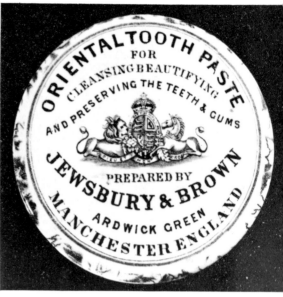

Pot lids for home and export markets. Jewsbury & Brown sold large quantities of their Oriental Tooth Paste throughout the nineteenth century.

to be equally well known in Europe, Asia, Africa, America and Australasia. The consumption must be enormous.' The diary was probably fictitious, but proof of the widespread distribution has come from dump-diggers in the United States, Canada, Australia, New Zealand, South Africa, India and Singapore who have all found the black and white lids used by Gosnell for the 'Extra Moist' variety of this 'globe-trotting' dentifrice.

Many other British-made black and white lids for toothpaste and cold creams have been found overseas. Almost all are varieties used by large manufacturers and wholesalers for packaging their branded products. Few colonial retailers had lids designed for their own makes of creams and pastes, perhaps because the

An advertisement dated 1910, by which time Jewsbury & Brown were beginning to favour toothpaste tubes.

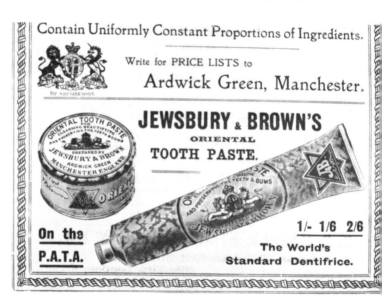

Contain Uniformly Constant Proportions of Ingredients.

Write for PRICE LISTS to
Ardwick Green, Manchester.

JEWSBURY & BROWN'S
ORIENTAL
TOOTH PASTE.

On the
P.A.T.A.

1/- 1/6 2/6

The World's
Standard Dentifrice.

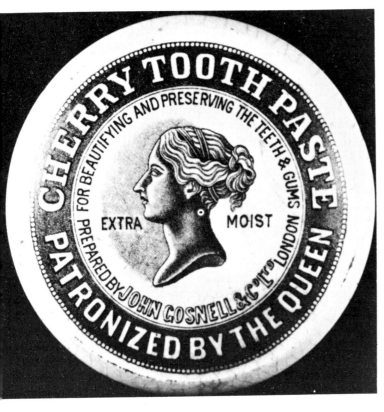

The 'Extra Moist' black and white lid known to diggers throughout the world.

expense was too great or perhaps because their customers pre-ferred to 'buy British' and to be reminded when they cleaned their teeth or applied cold cream to their faces of the old country thousands of miles away.

Competition

Thus was the black and white pot lid industry sustained and encouraged to grow during the last twenty years of the nine-teenth century. After 1900, competition against earthenware pots mounted relentlessly. Sales of boxes made in grease-proofed cardboard increased; pots made from cork were offered as alternatives to earthenware; tin boxes decorated with colour printing were widely advertised. Most serious for the potteries were the invention of the collapsible toothpaste tube and the rise in popularity of tooth powders which were dry and could be easily packaged in other materials. Sales of toothpastes in earthenware pots accounted for ninety per cent of all the pot-teries' business in transfer-printed chemists' sundries by this time. When that market declined the pot lid industry was doomed.

Three miniature Gosnell pot lids, only 1¼ in. diameter. The one on the left is a very rare 'Free Sample' lid.

The end was a fade-out rather than a sudden disappearance. When large contracts from wholesalers stopped coming in a few potteries went back to the production of transfer-printed lids without makers' or retailers' names which they sold in small quantities to individual chemists. One or two abandoned trans-

19

Gosnell's bronze lids are rather dark and do not photograph well on black and white film. This problem seems to have given trouble in the company's late nineteenth-century advertisements.

fer-printing and turned out plain pots which either had paper labels fixed with waterproof glue or were used for the packaging of dry goods. They were used by a few traditional family chemists up to the 1930s. Lids with 'burnt-in' labels died out at least ten years earlier.

Other pot users

Throughout the transfer-printing era most of the pots produced were used by chemists and druggists, but a small trade was always carried on between the potteries and manufacturers of fish and meat pastes, confectioners, and one or two other industries. Some beautiful transfer-printed pots with tall bodies were produced for Devonshire clotted cream makers, and many lavishly decorated transfer-printed earthenware bottles and flasks were made for brewers and whisky distillers.

These twentieth-century competitors – cardboard boxes, coloured tins, cork, and collapsible toothpaste tubes – eventually killed off the market for transfer-printed pots.

MISCELLANEOUS BOXES.

One of the last fish- and meat-paste manufacturers to use transfer-printed pots was Sainsbury's, the well-known provisions merchants. Up to the 1920s the company sold potted meats and bloater pastes in earthenware pots bearing a trade mark and the words 'potted meat' or 'bloater paste'. The lids were plain and carried a coloured paper label. Most of the fish- and meat-paste makers abandoned transfer-printed lids long before 1920, though John Burgess & Son continued to sell their anchovy paste in a pot with a 'burnt-in' label long after toothpaste makers had turned to tubes and tins. This lid, which bears a coat-of-arms, remained unchanged for almost one hundred years. The lettering was only slightly altered when the company moved from its old premises in the Strand to a new factory at Willesden at the beginning of the twentieth century.

Apart from John Burgess, the few fish- and meat-paste

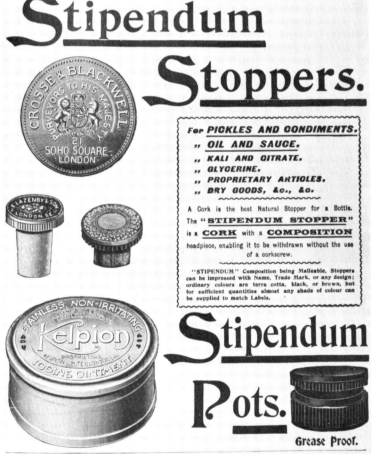

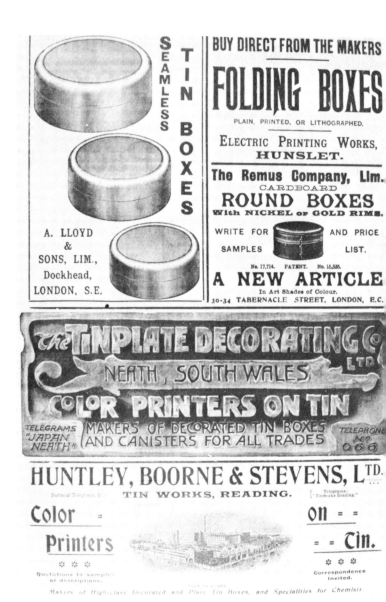
makers who did use transfer-printed lids after 1900 probably purchased standard designs without makers' names or trade marks. One such lid, found in many early twentieth century dumps, has a circular transfer bearing the words, 'an excellent relish for breakfast, luncheon, etc.' A horizontal section across the middle of the transfer is printed with the pot's contents: anchovy paste, bloater paste or potted meat. (See p. 108). On some examples this section was left blank so that the paste-maker could stick on a paper label describing his product.

Shape of pots

During more than a century of popularity, transfer-printed earthenware pots underwent several changes in shape and style which were dictated by methods of production and the needs

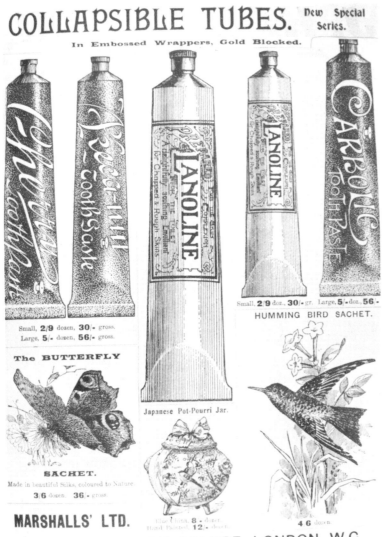
their lids were insecure. The paper band wrapped and glued of those industries that used them. The earliest pots were simple, straight-sided cylinders with flat and rimless lids. They were made on traditional potters' wheels and, although quite functional, their appearance was rather commonplace. The flat lid was ideally suited to the use of a paper label, but those potteries pioneering transfer printing – especially colour printing – required more attractive pots on which to display their work. Examples of colour-printed flat lids are very rare, though they were used in small numbers for black and white transfers throughout the nineteenth century.

Moulds and dies came into general use in the 1840s and firms such as F. & R. Pratt were soon turning out large colour-printed pots with slightly domed lids over four inches in diameter. This rapidly became the standard shape for colour printed lids which

Burgess's Victorian lids show the company's address as 107 Strand. Early twentieth-century lids *(right)* include the company's Willesden address in their transfers.

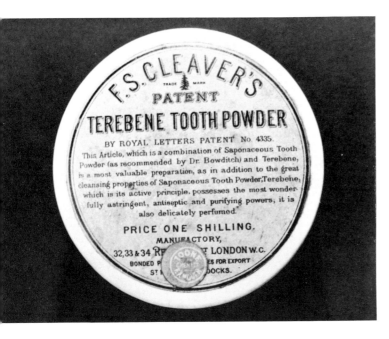

were generally much larger than black and whites. Very few coloured lids less than three inches in diameter were made, probably because engravers like Jesse Austin needed large lids to do justice to the subjects they chose to illustrate on them.

Freed of the need to use traditional wheels, potters could now mould 'patch boxes' with angular shapes as easily as they had previously made cylindrical containers. Square and oblong pots were made in large numbers, but they were never widely used for transfer-printed work. Only two or three oblong coloured pot lids are known, and more than ninety-five per cent of black and white lids are circular. The majority of black and white lid makers adopted smaller versions of the slightly domed round lid used for colour work as their standard until the 1890s when a few of the larger wholesale chemists began to favour square and oblong lids for their branded toothpastes and cold creams.

Another practice to enjoy a brief vogue in the 1890s was that of printing a transfer on the underside as well as the top of a lid. Large manufacturing chemists, eager to promote sales of even more products, instructed their pot-makers to print advertisements for soap and other toilet articles on the undersides of their toothpaste pot lids. Thus, a user of Cracroft's Toothpaste was reminded whenever he took the lid off the pot that he could also obtain from his local chemist a tablet of Sulpholine Soap – 'the purest, safest, best, and least expensive toilet soap' – at sixpence a bar. Some manufacturers also impressed advertisements into the pot's contents to catch the eye of any user who failed to turn the lid upside down.

A major disadvantage from which all earthenware pots suffered, and one which was never successfully overcome, was that

The domed shape of this Vinolia Shaving Soap lid is typical of many pot lids, both coloured and black and white. Note impressed advertisement in the pot's contents.

Earthenware pots of various shapes illustrated in a wholesaler's catalogue dated 1890.

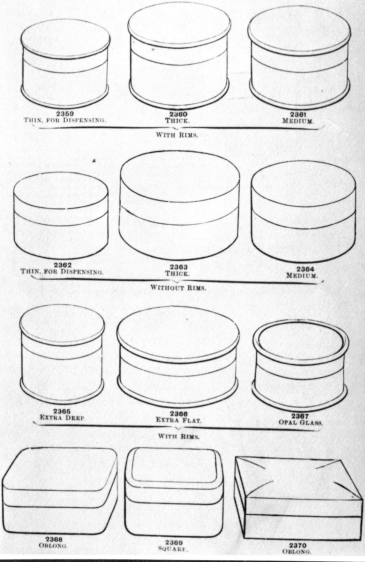

Two uncommon pot-lid shapes. The oval lid is very rare; the oblong version not widely used.

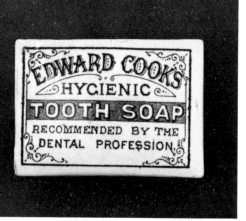

their lids were insecure. The paper band wrapped and glued around the body of the pot held on the lid and was removed or torn to open the pot. If it became loose during storage on the shop's shelves the lid could easily fall off. It was this disadvantage that probably encouraged some manufacturers to adopt square and oblong pots during the period of massive toothpaste sales towards the end of the nineteenth century. A flat-sided pot could have its lid additionally secured with string.

It was difficult to tie string around a cylindrical pot, but this problem was overcome shortly before 1900 by a manufacturer named William Toogood of London. Toogood's round pots were made with notches on their bases and lids which held the string securely. They were also made in extra-thin earthenware to reduce their weight. As the inventor stated in his advertisements, this made them 'specially adapted for sending by post'. Unfortunately their invention came very late in the history of transfer printing and very few were produced with 'burnt-in' labels. Toogood was one of the few earthenware pot manufacturers who stamped his products with trade marks. The bases of all his pots have the words 'Toogood's Patent' printed on them. C. T. Maling of Newcastle, who made most of the transfer-printed earthenware marmalade jars for Keillers of Dundee, also marked his pots with the company's name. The only other names and trade marks so far recorded on the bases of black and white printed pots are those of the manufacturing and wholesale chemists who commissioned the lid transfers. Pots with the word 'Maw' incised on their bases, for example, were made for Maw, Son & Thompson (later Maw, Son & Sons), the well-known wholesale chemists. Ayrton & Saunders, Liverpool wholesalers, stamped the bases of their pots with the trade mark, 'IXL'.

Maw, Son & Sons, one of the largest wholesale chemists in the 1890s, adopted square pots for their branded toothpastes at about that time.

The paper band wrapped around the body of the pot helped to secure the lid. The band was torn to open the pot.

Victorian salesmanship

Nowadays shoppers enjoy a measure of protection against sharp practices by manufacturers intent on selling goods by subterfuge. No such protection was afforded Victorian customers who were obliged to contend with widespread deception and fraud whenever they went on a shopping expedition. A pot of bear's grease might well contain a high proportion of mutton fat disguised by perfumes and artificial colouring; testimonials from doctors and members of the aristocracy extolling the properties of a little-known brand of face cream were more than likely to have been written by the manufacturer; and pots transfer-printed with the name and trade mark of a reputable company were often re-used as packages for inferior products. Such sales methods were common in Victorian Britain, as is shown by the numerous advertisements placed by reputable companies in newspapers and magazines to warn customers against 'spurious imitations'.

A transfer design used by one company on its pot lids was often copied by other companies. Some merely imitated type

Advertisement transfer-printed on the underside of a lid.

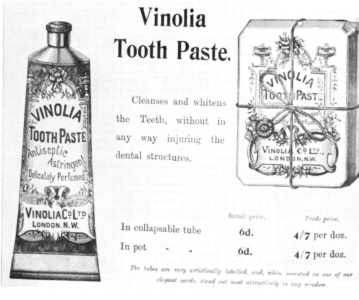

This advertisement for Vinolia Tooth Paste shows how lids had to be secured with string if pots were to be stood on their sides.

styles or borrowed words and phrases; but many copies so closely resembled the original that a shopper who did not look very carefully at the lid of the product he was buying could easily have bought an entirely different brand. These copies must not be confused with the standard lids wholesale chemists had made for their retailers which are always identical apart from the name and address of the retailers. Copies made by other companies were, of course, printed from different copper plates and their engravers always altered small details in the picture or design so that they could not be accused of making exact copies.

Collectors have also noted minor variations in lids which had a long run of popularity because the product sold well over

Advertisement for Toogood's pots dated 1900.

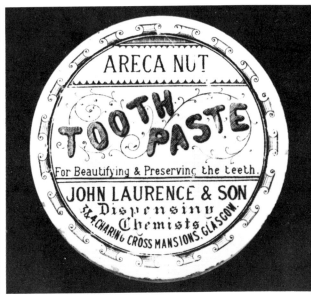

An example of one company borrowing a style of lettering from another.

These lids were made for two quite different companies, but they are so alike that many Victorian shoppers must have bought one thinking it was the other.

many years. These slight changes occurred when copper plates were re-engraved after becoming worn. At such times an engraver would take the opportunity to modify one or two details in the transfer – perhaps by altering a border or introducing new shading in the picture. New engravings were also made when a company changed its trading name or business address.

A widespread deception practised by everyone who manufactured and used transfer-printed earthenware pots was to make them appear to hold considerably more than they did. Bases were usually far thicker than was really necessary and often dome-shaped to reduce the size of the cavity inside the pot which was to be filled with the product. Lids were also given wide rims which overhung the body of the pot so that the container seemed much bigger. These sales methods must have succeeded because they were practised for more than a century; but many customers must often have wondered why their toothpaste or potted shrimps never seemed to last as long as they had expected when they bought the pot.

Claims to royal patronage were equally widespread and there can be little doubt that many were false. If evidence from transfer-printed lids is to be believed Queen Victoria used half a dozen brands of toothpaste and Prince Albert must have spent most of his day shaving with the assortment of soaps and creams manufacturers insisted he used. Eventually claims that members of the royal family used a product became so commonplace that some manufacturers turned to other famous people when seeking (or thinking up) patrons. W. Woods of Plymouth, maker of a very popular toothpaste, advertised in the 1890s that his 'Areca Nut' brand was 'used by Madame Marie Roze, the Prima Donna'.

Only future digging evidence will reveal the extent to which the late Victorian pot lid industry grew. Records such as illustrated catalogues showing the range of transfers each manufacturer or wholesaler could offer to retail chemists have not survived; nor does anyone know how many potteries were involved in the trade. There can be no doubt that every retail chemist in business between 1880 and 1900 sold a range of products in transfer-printed pots. Some restricted their stocks to the brands available from wholesalers, but a large number of enterprising retailers must have seen the advertising benefits to be gained from a pot lid indelibly printed with their own name and address which would have remained in a customer's possession for several days or weeks before it was relegated to the dustbin. There was no National Health Service in those days and even the smallest town or village had one or two chemist's shops which must each have sold hundreds of items packaged in earthenware pots every year. It follows that every accessible nineteenth century rubbish dump in Britain contains pot lids which, when recovered, will add to our knowledge of the subject. As will be explained in the next chapter, there are some dumps which contain exceptionally large numbers of pot lids.

Top row opposite :
Minor changes in border design on two Otto of Rose Cold Cream lids. Issued by S. F. Goss.

Middle row opposite :
A change of company name: S. Maw, Son & Thompson became S. Maw, Son & Sons in 1897.

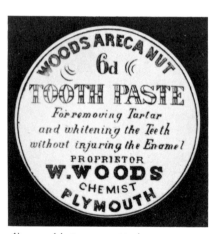

Above and bottom row opposite :
Transfer variations on Wood's Areca Nut pot lids.

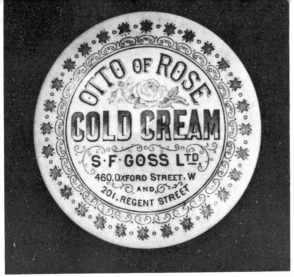

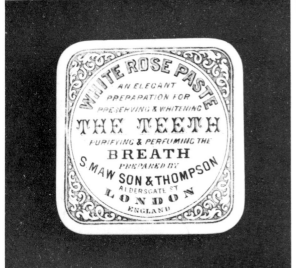

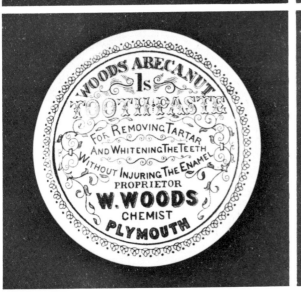

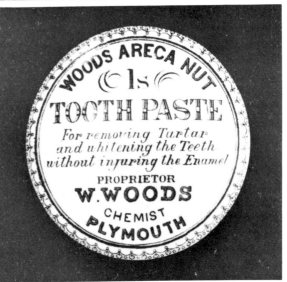

Opposite and middle row:
Transfer variations on Atkinson's Rose Cold Cream. Note differences in the curved lines around the word 'Rose'.

Bottom row:
A complete change of transfer for Lewis & Burrow's Areca Nut Tooth Paste – made when the company changed its trading name from Lewis & Burrows Ltd to Lewis & Burrows Drug Stores Ltd at the end of the nineteenth century.

2 Where to look for pot lids

In my earlier books, *Bottle Collecting* and *Digging up Antiques*, I urged readers hoping to find Victorian rubbish dumps to carry out searches within a few miles of their homes. The advice was sound because those books are concerned with the recovery of a variety of Victorian containers and other discarded objects found on any site containing household refuse dumped during the previous century. No matter where you live, the nineteenth century dump in your district will contain *some* earthenware pots with 'burnt-in' labels because, as explained in the previous chapter, they were sold in every city, town and village in Britain during that period. Small collections of lids found on local sites are owned by most bottle collectors who look upon them as a bonus earned during the more serious business of recovering bottles, and who are satisfied to find half a dozen in an entire season of digging.

I am sure newcomers to pot lid collecting will be delighted with that recovery rate and, once again, I urge them to make a start by seeking sites close to home on which to gain digging experience and to find their first lids. The advantages of doing so include easier access to historical records which will indicate likely sites, and much shorter journeys to and from a dump when digging commences. The methods used to locate and dig sites discussed later in this chapter apply to all dumps and will be found equally useful to beginners seeking their first local site and to experienced diggers tracking down dumps further afield.

Rubbish dump contents

Dedicated pot lid hunters whose searches have taken them to many parts of Britain know that lids are not equally distributed throughout all dumps and that the contents of a nineteenth century dump in one area can be quite different to the contents of a dump of similar age in another part of the country. This is equally true of modern dumps. A few years ago an enterprising market research organization hit upon the novel idea of searching people's dustbins in order to learn more about their buying habits. By adding up the marked prices on throwaway containers and wrappings in a dustbin the researchers were able to assess fairly accurately the percentage of income each family spent on groceries and their preferences whenever there was a choice between one brand of food and another. After months of sifting and sorting, the researchers announced their general conclusion: families with higher incomes spent more on food than families with low incomes and usually bought more expensive brands than their less fortunate neighbours.

In fairness to the researchers it must be said that they did learn rather more than this; they were, for instance, able to conclude that when a product was packaged in a carton of one colour it sold better than when the carton was of a different colour. Specific information on each family's buying habits was also far more accurate when obtained from the contents of its dustbin than when the housewife was asked face-to-face questions by an interviewer. Nevertheless, the general conclusion is certainly less than a revelation. The better-off have always eaten well; the poor have made do with what they could afford.

In Victorian society divisions between the better-off and the poor were far more pronounced than they are today. Had the market researchers been able to look into dustbins filled in the 1870s they would have reached the same conclusion they arrived at in the 1970s, but the research would have taken only a few days. The poor threw away little more than ashes from the fire, one or two broken clay tobacco pipes, and a few bottles on which no deposit was charged. Their refuse contained no empty toothpaste pots because even at sixpence a pot toothpaste was a luxury they could not afford. They cleaned their teeth with a damp piece of cloth dipped in soot. Nor were bear's grease and delicately perfumed cold cream on the weekly shopping lists of working class families in the late nineteenth century.

True, they ate considerably more fish and meat paste than families in higher income groups, but they made their purchases 'down the market' from open stalls where fishmongers and butchers sold freshly made pastes by the quarter-pound. These were not packaged at all; after weighing they were taken from the scales and placed in the buyer's own dish or basin specially brought to the market for that purpose. (Even today in some northern towns with large working-class populations fish and meat pastes, hot pies and peas, brawn, udder and tripe are still sold in this way.)

The middle and upper classes lived quite different lives and their dustbins were filled to overflowing with the refuse of affluence – bottles with glass seals bearing the impressed trade marks of local wine merchants, ornate clay tobacco pipes thrown out only because their bowls had become stained, green glass jars that had held pickles and preserves, empty sauce bottles made from pale blue glass, earthenware blacking pots emptied by the maids as they sweated to bring a shine to the kitchen stove, and a rich assortment of toothpaste, cold cream and paste pots. Class privilege was not the sole reason for the efficient refuse-collection service provided by the local corporations for

uch households; the volume of rubbish they produced made
an efficient service absolutely essential.

The best towns for pot lids

There were, of course, no Victorian cities or towns with populations made up entirely of upper and middle-class citizens; but
there were many in industrial Lancashire, the West Riding of
Yorkshire, County Durham, the coal-mining regions of Central
Scotland, the Staffordshire Potteries, South Wales and Cornwall
where poor working-class families vastly outnumbered those
with sufficient income to afford a few luxuries. Pot lid finds
in most dumps in these counties are consequently scarce. They
are equally scarce for different reasons in the Highlands of Scotland, the border counties of northern England, the Yorkshire
moorlands, much of Lincolnshire, Norfolk and Suffolk, and
large areas of the Midlands which at that time had not been
eaten up by industrial growth. These regions had mainly agricultural economies, small populations and few retail shops. Sales
of packaged goods other than bottled beers and spirits were,
therefore, never very large.

In many cities and towns outside the industrial regions mentioned above there were also large working-class populations,
but in some of these conurbations the better-off had, by the
1880s, segregated themselves from the lower orders by moving
to residential areas on the outskirts of the cities. In the early
years of the Industrial Revolution most of the new manufacturers had lived as close as possible to their factories. As these
factories grew in size it became increasingly important to house
workers close to them so that the hours of work could be as
long as possible. This rapidly produced overcrowded slums in
the central areas and those who could afford to do so moved
away to escape the smoke and grime. At the time of the Great
Exhibition of 1851, when F. & R. Pratt and T. J. & J. Mayer
displayed their first coloured pot lids, London was an overcrowded and unhealthy city of two million souls. The manufacturers, merchants, most important shopkeepers, and better-paid
civil servants and clerks had already departed – some as far
as Staines and Virginia Water – to become London's first com-
muters.

Cities and towns which were important administrative or cultural centres where civil servants, office workers, university staff
and other 'white collar' workers swelled the ranks of the middle
classes, and which did not grow in size only because of an influx
of unskilled factory workers, are likely to have late nineteenth
century rubbish dumps containing a high proportion of pot lids.
The larger the city the more likely is it that refuse collected
from better-class residential areas was dumped at different sites
to those used for the disposal of refuse from poorer quarters,
the reason for this being the appreciable distance separating
the two groups. Thus, in London, refuse from the East End
was disposed of along the banks of the Thames in Essex and

Kent, while rubbish collected on the western side of the city – and which contained many more pot lids – was dumped in clay pits along the sides of the Grand Union Canal from Brentford to Slough.

Cities and towns with large middle class populations in the late nineteenth century:

London, Edinburgh, Bristol, Oxford, Cambridge, Canterbury Winchester, Gloucester, Lincoln, Norwich, York.

Note: London is a special case because of its size and because excellent rail services made possible the conversion of large areas of North Surrey and East Berkshire into residential suburbs for the middle classes from 1850 onwards. Excellent pot lid dumps can be found in these counties today in addition to those along canal banks north-west of the city.

Seaside resorts

Nowadays annual holidays are taken for granted; very few families fail to 'get away from it all' for a few weeks in summertime and an increasing number are able to afford two holidays each year. A century ago things were quite different. The working classes got no paid holidays; Monday to Saturday working and fourteen-hour shifts were common in most factories where owners firmly believed leisure for the masses inevitably resulted in drunkeness, sabotage and riot. For the middle classes, on the other hand, the annual holiday had, by the 1880s, become a social obligation. More adventurous and richer families headed for month-long Continental tours; the conservative but equally rich preferred traditional spas such as Bath, Tonbridge or Harrogate; the less well-off – the vast majority of middle-class citizens were far from rich – chose one of the popular seaside resorts where they could combine the enjoyment of promenade concerts with the medicinal benefits of a plunge in the sea. To reach their destinations they took a train.

The railways made swift and economical travel possible for millions in the nineteenth century, and no recreational activity was more popular with middle-class Victorians than a trip to the coast by train. Brighton, connected by a direct line with the capital in 1841, was the first choice for holiday-making Londoners. In the eighteenth century, when the coach fare was twenty-one shillings return, Brighton had been popular with fashionable society led by the Prince of Wales. They went there to visit the bathing establishment founded by Doctor Richard Russell of Lewes, who advocated a dip in the ocean as a cure for all manner of ailments. By 1845 railways had reduced the normal fare to ten shillings return and excursion trains with fares reduced to as little as five shillings were carrying up to four thousand passengers on each trip. The aristocratic patrons departed and the middle classes arrived to take their place.

Brighton Pier in the 1870s. These were the customers who bought shrimp paste in pots with coloured lids.

Hundreds of hotels and guest houses were built, theatres flourished, and the promenades were taken over by the daughters of clerks and shopkeepers showing off their new gowns to smartly dressed young men with dandified walking canes. On the beaches, those not taking a medicinal plunge from a bathing machine hunted pebbles and fossils or sat beneath their sunshades with telescopes and copies of *The Times*. Brighton's shops did a roaring trade in all manner of souvenirs, knick-knacks and delicacies. Potted shrimps in coloured pots from Pegwell Bay were firm favourites, but many other fish and meat pastes in earthenware pots sold almost as well to families planning picnics on the beach. Chemists were also kept busy selling pots of toothpaste to hotel guests and cold creams to young ladies who had caught too much sun.

The success of the Brighton line – the first in Britain built primarily to serve and develop a holiday resort – encouraged railway companies to put down tracks to other seaside towns. Soon Ramsgate, Margate and Broadstairs – the first seaside resort described in its advertising as 'select' and a firm favourite with Charles Dickens – were attracting London holiday-makers with offerings of potted shrimps, ornamental gardens, bathing machines and brass bands. By the late 1880s the coast from Thanet to the Solent was dotted with seaside towns served by a train service from London and competing with Brighton for holiday trade. Deal, Dover, Folkestone, Hastings, St Leonards, Eastbourne, Seaford, Worthing, Portsmouth, Southampton and Lymington all joined in. A few of the resorts closer to London were now within reach of the working classes who crowded into Sunday excursion trains to enjoy a once-in-a-lifetime breath of sea air and a donkey ride on the sands at Margate or Ramsgate, though the majority of London's East Enders preferred Southend. The middle classes, ever conscious of the need to remain 'select' began to take their holidays further westward or boarded the ferries to the Isle of Wight's resorts at Cowes, Ventnor, Ryde and Shanklin.

Further afield, Bournemouth did not begin to develop as a popular holiday spot until the last decade of the nineteenth century, and even then its progress as a resort was slow. The town's central station was opened in 1899, but Bournemouth's reputation was that of a convalescent centre for consumptives and it was not until the early years of the twentieth century that large numbers of holiday-makers arrived. Sales of potted shrimps in coloured pots had ceased by that time, but the town's chemists sold large quantities of toothpaste, shaving cream and cold cream in transfer-printed pots up to the early 1920s.

Weymouth was the most important resort in Dorset and a popular watering place long before the railway age. (George III took his first dip in the sea here.) When the trains came in 1857, middle-class Victorians flocked to Weymouth from London, the Midlands and the West Country. Lyme Regis, the only other resort of any significance on that coast, lost much of its trade to Weymouth because it did not get a railway line until 1903.

The resorts of the South Devon coast – Sidmouth, Exmouth, Dawlish, Teignmouth and Torquay – had developed during the Napoleonic Wars when the Continent was temporarily closed to British travellers. When the railways came to Devon in the 1840s, Sidmouth was already a winter residence for many upper-class Victorians and the town's traders actively discouraged the building of a railway until 1874, fearing that newcomers would drive away the richer clientèle. Exmouth, another old-established resort, declined in the late 1840s when the South Devon Railway by-passed the town and carried visitors to Dawlish, Teignmouth and Torquay.

Of these three, Torquay was by far the most important resort. Between 1840 and 1870 its resident population increased from 6,000 to 22,000 and it was during those years that the well-planned terraces and villas familiar to visitors today were built. Since 1828 when the Royal Hotel was rebuilt and adapted 'for the reception of families of the first distinction' Torquay had concentrated on luring the rich; when the rich began to prefer holidays abroad the middle classes moved in.

Cornwall had no Victorian resorts and North Devon had only Ilfracombe which attracted some visitors from South Wales, still without seaside resorts, who came by steam packet across the Bristol Channel. In Somerset there was Weston-super-Mare, a famed health and pleasure resort long before the railway reached it in 1841. A forty-bedroom hotel had been built in Weston as early as 1808 and the town was renowned as the playground of Bristol's upper classes. The railway brought middle-class Londoners in their thousands throughout the Victorian era.

Although the annual seaside holiday was at first a southern institution it spread to the north after 1850. Cromer and Yarmouth attracted middle-class visitors from the Midlands; Scarborough, famous as a spa long before the Industrial Revolution, became the holiday-resort of mill owners and their families from the West Riding; Southport on the Lancashire coast and Aberystwyth in Cardiganshire prospered as holiday centres for the richer families of the cotton towns. In Scotland, Glasgow's middle classes could choose from Gourock in Renfrewshire, Dunoon in Argyllshire, or Rothesay in Buteshire. The citizens of Edinburgh went to North Berwick.

In all of these seaside towns, from Brighton in the south to Gourock in the north, sales of fish and meat pastes, toothpastes, shaving creams, cold creams and other products packaged in earthenware pots were enormous between 1880 and 1910. Their Victorian rubbish dumps abound with transferprinted lids and few of those sites outside Sussex and Kent have yet been extensively explored.

Victorian seaside resorts with excellent pot lid hunting dumps
KENT: Margate, Broadstairs, Ramsgate, Deal, Dover, Folkestone
SUSSEX: Hastings, St. Leonards, Eastbourne, Seaford, Brighton, Worthing
HAMPSHIRE: Portsmouth, Southampton, Lymington, Bournemouth
I.O.W.: Cowes, Ventnor, Ryde, Shanklin
DORSET: Weymouth
DEVON: Sidmouth, Dawlish, Teignmouth, Torquay
SOMERSET: Weston-super-Mare
NORFOLK: Cromer, Yarmouth
YORKSHIRE: Scarborough
LANCASHIRE: Southport
CARDIGANSHIRE: Aberystwyth
RENFREWSHIRE: Gourock
ARGYLLSHIRE: Dunoon
BUTESHIRE: Rothesay
EAST LOTHIAN: North Berwick

Spas
Inland resorts also prospered with the arrival of the railways, though they had long been popular with the upper classes in coaching days. All were spas, renowned for their curative waters

as much as their theatres, pleasure gardens, and fine buildings. It was sea-bathing and the growth of resorts on the coast that eventually brought about their decline, but they attracted large numbers of visitors throughout the pot lid era and their nineteenth-century dumps are rich in pot lid finds.

Most famous of all was Bath where the eighteenth-century aristocracy soothed their aches and pains in the waters and worked off the effects of gluttony and too much port while enjoying the city's social life. The Victorians, less inclined to over-eating and alcohol, visited Bath more for the delights of its public gardens, excellent hotels, and surrounding country-side. Many came to settle here with their families in the 1890s when its days of high fashion had drawn to a close.

Tunbridge Wells, closer to London, was a popular watering place as early as the seventeenth century when its patrons included Charles II and Queen Anne. In the nineteenth century Queen Victoria's frequent visits kept Tunbridge on the social map, and in the Edwardian era the borough was bestowed with the title of Royal Tunbridge Wells.

Buxton was advertised in the nineteenth century as 'the most bracing spa in the Kingdom', and it was the Derbyshire countryside as much as the town's hotels and mineral springs that attracted Victorian visitors. Matlock, in the same county, was equally popular and both resorts benefited much from the new railways which made the Peak District accessible to thousands of fascinated Victorians.

Cheltenham, Malvern, Droitwich and Leamington were the famous nineteenth-century resorts of the Midlands, much patronized by middle-class visitors from Birmingham and London. In Wales the spas were Llanwrtyd, Builth Wells and Llandrindod, which in the eighteenth century had attracted visitors from Swansea, Carmarthen and Cardiff. When the London and North Western Railway was built in 1866 these resorts were brought within reach of Londoners seeking salmon and trout fishing, delightful scenery and cures for their aches and pains. By 1900 the largest resort, Llandrindod, was attracting 80,000 visitors a year.

In Yorkshire the popularity of Scarborough as a seaside watering place was challenged after 1800 by the inland delights of Harrogate. Harrogate had been famous as a spa since the sixteenth century, but its baths, Pump Room and hotels were built in the early nineteenth century. When the mania for 'electric' cures took hold on Victorian imaginations after 1850 Harrogate used electric currents as part of its eighty methods of treating arthritis, gout, dyspepsia, anaemia, dysentry and the aftermath of tropical diseases. A Pullman rail service from London to Edinburgh made Harrogate its half-way stopping place, and at the resort's peak of popularity, one thousand people were treated for their ailments every day at the Royal Baths.

Ilkley, seventeen miles from Harrogate, was smaller but could trace its wells and baths back to Roman days. Like the larger resort, it enjoyed national popularity after the coming of the railway (in 1865), and by 1900 it was attracting 200,000 visitors a year. Although never visited by royalty it enjoyed the patronage of many famous Victorians, including Madame Tussaud.

The Lake District did not have its own spa at the beginning of the nineteenth century, but it did have the beginnings of a tourist trade. Hardier members of the upper classes were tackling the Lakeland fells on 'mountain ponies' before 1800; and when the town of Windermere was created by the building of a railway station in 1847, dukes and duchesses flocked in. Hotels were hurriedly built, the Royal Windermere Yacht Club was founded, and the society whirl got underway. The middle classes – businessmen, intellectuals, professors, doctors and clergymen – arrived in the 1860s and Windermere's hotels were soon accommodating thousands of visitors every year. To compete with Harrogate and Ilkley, Windermere built its own hydro (complete with Turkish baths) and ballroom, and established a ladies' orchestra.

North of the border Victorian spas were smaller but equally extravagant in their advertising claims. Moffat, in Dumfriesshire, styled itself 'the Scotch Baden-Baden'; Ballater, in Aberdeenshire, was 'patronized by Her Most Gracious Majesty Queen Victoria during her visits to Balmoral'; and Strathpeffer Spa, in Ross and Cromarty, had, in 1898, one hotel which included in its advertised ammenities 'a cycle court with professional attendants'.

These were Britain's inland resorts in the nineteenth century. Their lavishly stocked chemist's and grocer's shops sold tens of thousands of transfer-printed earthenware pots with coloured and black and white lids to free-spending, middle-class visitors during the latter half of the Victorian era and in some cases throughout the Edwardian era. The pots and their lids found their way via hotel and guest-house dustbins to rubbish dumps on the outskirts of town – and most of them have not yet been recovered.

Inland resorts popular in the nineteenth century
SOMERSET: Bath
KENT: Tunbridge Wells
DERBYSHIRE: Buxton, Matlock
WORCESTERSHIRE: Malvern, Droitwich
WARWICKSHIRE: Leamington
GLOUCESTERSHIRE: Cheltenham
RADNORSHIRE: Builth Wells, Llandrindod
BRECONSHIRE: Llanwrtyd
YORKSHIRE: Harrogate, Ilkley
WESTMORLAND: Windermere
DUMFRIESSHIRE: Moffat
ABERDEENSHIRE: Ballater
ROSS AND CROMARTY: Strathpeffer

The cities and towns mentioned in this chapter and shown on the map opposite offer the best prospects of substantial pot lid finds to all diggers, but they are most certainly not the only places in Britain where lids can be found. Local dumps dating from 1880 to 1910 are always worth investigating; even though pot lid finds will be fewer, the lids recovered might be rare examples. For the same reason a very small dump associated with a farm or an isolated house known to have been occupied by a middle-class family in the nineteenth century might prove as rewarding to a determined digger as any dump in one of the important cities or towns.

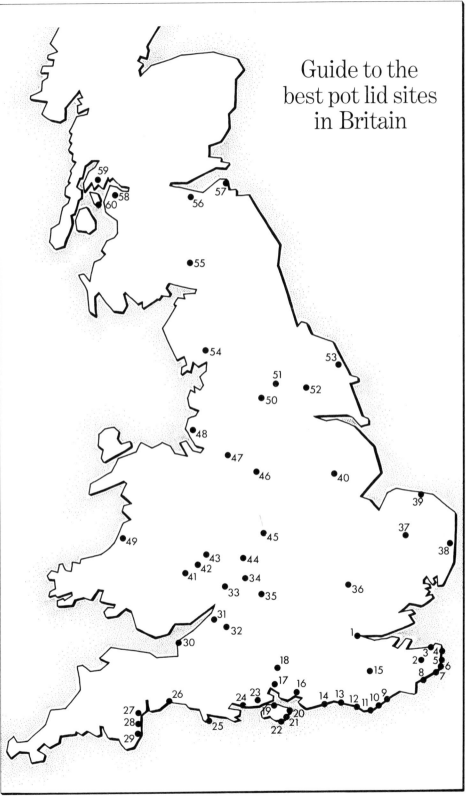

Guide to the best pot lid sites in Britain

3 Successful hunting

Beginners' mistakes

During the many years I have been interested in dump-digging I have met, talked with, and observed hundreds of pot lid hunters including raw beginners, professionals earning their livings at the game, and many enthusiastic collectors who own two or three hundred prize lids. The conclusions I have drawn from my observations and conversations with them are no more dramatic than those drawn by the market researchers mentioned at the beginning of this chapter; but the lessons to be learned from them are of the utmost importance to all readers who have yet to find and dig their first dump. The conclusions are:

1. Beginners are far more easily deterred by initial failures when attempting to locate a site than are more experienced dump diggers;

2. Beginners rarely dig deep enough when excavating a dump; because of this they miss many excellent finds.

The most successful dump-hunters are those prepared to cover long distances on foot. It is no coincidence that the man who has found more Victorian dumps than anyone else in Britain (John Webb of Hutton, Essex) cannot drive a car; nor is it a coincidence that people who attempt to locate sites while sitting behind steering wheels are those who go home empty handed. Cars cannot be used on dump-hunting expeditions – other than to reach the general area to be searched – because public roads rarely lead to Victorian refuse sites. Furthermore, many clues to the whereabouts of a dump are easily missed when travelling at even thirty miles per hour. A person on foot can examine the ground at leisure and interpret what he sees; a car driver must keep his eyes on the road and attempt to spot the clues by casting hurried glances from left to right. Inevitably these clues are missed.

There is another, less obvious disadvantage in using a car during a search for old dumps. The spot where the car is parked must be both the starting and finishing point of the search because the driver has to return to his car when his 'walkabout' comes to an end. The searcher on foot does not have to return to a starting point; he can catch a bus or train to the general area to be searched, walk five or ten miles in any direction, and return home by an entirely different route either on foot or by taking another bus or train. For these reasons I ask all beginners about to attempt finding their first local dump to leave their cars at home.

Equipment

If not a car what *do* you require on a dump-hunting expedition? I suggest a strong pair of shoes or walking boots, one-inch Ordnance Survey maps of the area ten miles around your home town, and a small and lightweight digging tool. You do not, at this stage, require tools to dig deeply into a dump; your initial aim is to confirm the location of the site, not to find pot lids. It is a serious mistake to overload yourself with equipment when you might have to walk five or ten miles to find a site. Excavation comes later; for the present you must strip the load to be carried to a minimum so that you do not become tired after walking a couple of miles. The only other items required are a notebook, pencil and possibly a few sandwiches and a flask of coffee.

Obtaining information on possible sites

Let me presume you have set aside one day of your weekend to find a dump and, taking my advice, have decided to leave your car in the garage. Firstly, you must allow yourself a complete day for the hunt; do not spend the morning in bed and hope to make up the time by hurrying in the afternoon. Leave the house early and go into the centre of town. The next hour or two should be spent wandering around the main shopping area on the lookout for as many old gentlemen as you can stop and talk with in that time! Ideally you must find several men aged eighty or more who have lived in the district all their lives and whose memories are still sharp.

This is by no means as difficult as it sounds. Every town in Britain has hundreds – in large cities possibly thousands – of residents who fit this description. The majority thoroughly enjoy talking about 'the old days' and you are sure to find most of them eager to help in your search for a site. The question you must ask after introducing yourself and explaining your interest in local history is: 'Do you recall where the town's household rubbish was dumped before the Great War?' A man of eighty (in 1974) would have been a boy of ten in 1914, and if he lived in the town at that time it is very likely that he visited the town's dump to look for Codd's bottles which he broke in order to increase his collection of glass marbles.

For the benefit of readers who are not bottle collectors let me explain that a Codd's bottle is a glass mineral water bottle with a crimped neck in which a marble is trapped. The marble acted as a stopper when the bottle was filled with lemonade; gas in the liquid held the marble tightly at the top of the neck until pressure was released by forcing the marble downwards to allow the gas to escape. They are known as Codd's bottle after Hiram Codd, their inventor, and they were used throughout Britain from the 1870s until the 1920s. (For further information see my earlier books, *Bottle Collecting* and *Digging up Antiques*).

If you are already a bottle collector and you have a Codd' bottle, take it with you on this expedition. It will help enormously to jog the memory of any old gentleman you talk to. His eyes will probably light up when he sees it and he might soon be telling you where he broke off the necks of such bottle as a boy. Produce your map at this point and attempt to get an accurate fix on the spot he recalls as having been the dump in those days. It is also worthwhile to ask if he remember where rubbish was dumped before that particular site was used and where it was dumped when that site had been filled with refuse. Mark every location given on your map – even if the old gentleman insists that the sites are now covered by housing estates, factories, office blocks or playing fields. You should also make notes on any details about rubbish collection and disposal your informant provides, for example, how the rubbish was taken to the site, what the site was used for before it became a refuse tip, and any other relevant facts.

Having obtained these details from one source you must now confirm them by finding more old people and listening carefully to their comments and opinions on the subject. Each time a site is suggested mark it on your map and add to your note every scrap of information given about refuse disposal in your town during the Edwardian era. If, during your first morning as a dump-hunter, you can talk to half a dozen octogenarian who spent their youth in your town, by noon you will be very knowledgeable about local refuse disposal history and well on your way to finding that first dump.

Looking for dumps

Your next task is to check out the sites marked on your map. If you have more than one, work out a logical route to include them all and decide which you will visit first. There is no objection to taking a bus to the outskirts of town at this stage as nothing much is gained by walking through built-up areas; nor is anything lost by riding in comfort along major roads that bring you closer to the site.

Sites used as rubbish dumps before 1914 fall into three categories:

1. Holes in the ground made during the excavation of clay, sand, gravel or chalk which were filled with rubbish after excavation work ceased;
2. Land reclamation schemes in which household refuse was used to raise the level of low-lying marshland on seacoasts or on riversides;
3. Brickworks to which rubbish was taken for use in the brickmaking process.

Two methods were used to transport the rubbish to these sites:

1. Horse-drawn carts which hauled their loads from the town along public roads and cart tracks leading to the dumping ground;
2. Barges which were loaded in or near the town with cartloads of rubbish and which then carried their cargoes to the dumping ground along rivers and canals. Here each cargo was off-loaded into small hand-barrows which could be man-handled to the final dumping point.

Your earlier conversations with old people will have indicated the type of site used in your town and the transportation method employed. If carts were used, the first clues to look for are tracks leading from public roads in the general direction of a spot marked on your map as a possible dump. Leave the bus when you reach a point within a mile or two of the suspected site and look on your Ordnance Survey map for dotted lines indicating footpaths, tracks or bridleways across fields. Those with public rights of way are indicated by red dots or broken lines; private tracks are coloured black on the map, but few people will object to your use of them if you take care to shut all gates, avoid damaging crops and fences, and respect the other rules of the Country Code.

Those paths which have stiles across them where they join public roads can be eliminated immediately as possible routes to a dump; look instead for those with wide, and sometimes gated entrances sufficiently wide to permit passage of a horse-drawn cart. If the track shows signs of long and hard use in the past and it is deeply rutted on its edges but overgrown with grass and weeds across its middle it is very likely to be the track you are seeking. Walk along it as far as possible and check both sides for evidence that it was used by carts carrying

Track used by horse-drawn carts to carry refuse to a dump. It was raised above the level of the field by laying a foundation of ashes, glass and pottery fragments.

household refuse – small pieces of broken pottery, odd bottles or ashes which might have fallen from the loads. Often these tracks were made by laying down solid materials such as glass, pottery and cinders taken from the loads, and fragments can sometimes be seen in the rutted areas at the edges. By following this track to its end you should reach the dump, but it is unlikely you will there be confronted with mounds of pot lids and other refuse. If the original site was a hole in the ground it was probably covered by two feet of soil when filled; the surface might now be farmland or an overgrown tangle of weeds.

One of the advantages of carrying out searches for old rubbish dumps in wintertime is that sites such as this are either ploughed over and have no crops growing on them, or the natural vegetation has died off to leave the surface of the ground partly visible. If the site of the dump has been reclaimed as farmland and you are visiting it in the spring or summer you will see nothing but a field of wheat or vegetables. If, on the other hand, you are seeking the dump during the months from November to early March you will see large amounts of broken

Elders growing on a Victorian refuse dump. The photograph was taken in winter; it shows clearly the dry, dead branches and gnarled bark of the trees – a certain indication that the ground here contains large amounts of ashes and cinders.

ottery and glass that have come to the surface during plough-
ng, or you will spot similar objects in the roots of any dead
egetation covering the site.

Examining the site

No dump-digging can be carried out in the spring or summer
if the site is covered by growing crops; but if the site has not
been reclaimed for agricultural use you must now examine the
vegetation growing on it. When this consists largely of hawthorn
bushes and healthy-looking grass it is likely that the dump has
been covered to a considerable depth by clay. This was sometimes done when a hole was only partly filled with refuse: to
avoid wastage of good topsoil a layer of clay, and sometimes
brick rubble, was used to level the site. In such a case recovery
of pot lids or any other objects deposited in the dump will
be extremely difficult; I suggest you look elsewhere for a digging
site. If the vegetation consists largely of elders, (which have
gnarled and very dry branches) nettles, brambles and coarse
grass they indicate well-drained soil beneath which a rubbish
dump is most likely to be found.

Often it is quite unnecessary to disturb the surface of the
site to confirm the presence of a dump beneath it. The area
will be dotted with rabbit holes, and if the material these animals bring to the surface while burrowing contains glass and
pottery these will be seen around the holes. If you cannot find
a rabbit hole it is only necessary to cut away some grass with
your digging tool and to scrape out the soil to a depth of twelve
inches in order to check whether or not the site contains broken
glass and pottery. If it does you have found your first dump.

Canalside dumps

Many Victorian and Edwardian rubbish dumps located in
former clay pits are sited alongside canals. The pits were made
when clay was extracted during eighteenth and nineteenth-century canal construction to provide an impervious layer on the
bed of the canal. In the late nineteenth century a use was found
for these holes as convenient rubbish disposal sites. The canals
provided a cheap means of transport from town to dump and
large numbers of barges were employed on this work between
1880 and 1920. If your town lies on a canal route it is almost
certain that some of the sites suggested by the old men you
talk to will be on canalsides a few miles from town. They can
easily be found by walking along the towpaths and looking for
areas of dense undergrowth including nettles, brambles and
elders. Often derelict moorings will indicate the exact spots
where barges unloaded their cargoes and the presence of the
dump can be quickly confirmed by a brief trial dig.

Land reclamation dumps

If your conversations in town suggest that refuse was used for
land reclamation schemes, then the dump you are seeking will

Typical canalside scene. A hundred years ago dozens of barges loaded with household refuse would have passed beneath this bridge every day on their way to dumps in disused clay pits along the canal.

lie alongside a river, a creek or a seashore. Land reclaimed i this way was once subject to flooding and most of the flood occurred near river mouths or on coasts that are not backe by cliffs. The work of reclaiming the marshes usually went o for many years (it continues today in some parts of the country and vast areas were made suitable for agricultural and industri use in this way. The problem in such a case is not to fin the dump, which is usually so large it cannot be missed, bu to find the areas within it that were reclaimed before 1914 This is made much easier if accurate locations can be obtaine during your conversations with the men who knew the site in their boyhood. Phrases such as, 'somewhere on the marshe or 'down by the rivermouth' are much too vague. Encourag your informants to recall important details, such as the distanc from a prominent landmark to the dumping ground, or th name of a creek used by the refuse barges when taking thei cargoes to the site. If you are very lucky you might persuad one of the old men to accompany you on your expedition, per haps after you have bought him a few pints of ale at the loc pub!

In the absence of an accurate location, the Ordnance Surve map often provides useful clues. In all areas where low-lyin land has been reclaimed the riverside or coast will be protecte by embankments which hold back the water when its level i raised by tides or flooding. These features are shown on th map as two rows of short black lines looking rather like a serie of inverted commas. On former marshland they are also ofte found some distance inland from the modern riverside wher they mark the line of the riverbank as it was at some tim in the past. In order to reclaim land by dumping, an embank ment of stones is first made to hold back the river or sea, an the waterlogged land *behind* the embankment is then filled wit refuse until its level is raised above that of the water. To reclaim more land another embankment is constructed on the tidal fore hore and the level of the land between the first embankment and the second is again raised by dumping. The reclaiming of large areas of land might involve building several embankments over a period of a century or more, and even though the older embankments are rendered obsolete they are not destroyed because they act as reserve lines of defence in times of flood.

The reclamation of land by this method has been carried on in Britain since Roman times, but it was in the late Victorian period, when vast amounts of household rubbish were being produced by expanding cities and towns, that the most ambitious projects were undertaken. Those embankments shown on your Ordnance Survey map as farthest from the present-day riverbank or coastline are most likely to be Victorian constructions and it is behind them that the most productive pot lid sites are to be found. Sometimes rubbish was transported to these embankments by horse-drawn carts, but barges were far more widely employed. They usually reached the site by travelling down the main river and then along a tidal creek to bring them as close as possible to the embankment. Wooden staithes were erected on the banks of the creek and the refuse was discharged from the barges into hand-barrows which were wheeled along the embankment to the dump. Derelict staithes and discarded hand-barrows can sometimes be seen on the beds of dried-out creeks in these areas – a sure sign that there is a dump nearby.

Vegetation

Because reclaimed land remains damp for many years the vegetation growing on Victorian refuse in these areas differs from the vegetation normally found on inland dumps. Elders rarely grow on them, though they sometimes flourish on the old embankments which, being raised above the general level, are usually much drier. Nettles are also far less common unless

Old embankment behind which Victorian refuse was dumped to reclaim the marshes.

Reeds growing on an old dump near a river estuary.

the site is a fair distance from water, or the dump is of excep tional depth. Dry reeds and thistles are the usual types of veg tation, though on former marshes now used for sheep and catt grazing the animals often eat or trample them. Large areas a often covered by short, springy grass which gives no clue a dump lying beneath it, but if hawthorn bushes are seen th means that there is a considerable depth of clay and dump-dig ging can be ruled out.

Brickworks dumps

Only very old men who can recall childhood life in the la nineteenth century will tell you that the town's household refus was used to make bricks, because the practice had largely die out by 1900. From 1850 to 1880 many brickworks purchase from local corporations household ashes which were mixed wit clay to make common bricks. Often the brickmakers owned the own fleets of barges or carts which they used to transport ash to their works from large collection centres in town where th rubbish had been sorted and the ash extracted by corporatio employees. The money brickmakers paid for the ashes covere the costs of the refuse collection service provided for the town citizens and very often a corporation would make a profit o the sales. After 1880 fewer bricks were made in this way an many corporations, faced with increasing amounts of unwante refuse, found that they could only get rid of their problem b giving the ashes to brickmakers without payment. In return the brickmakers agreed to accept unsorted refuse which they screened to extract ash at their own works. It was during this period that the collection of dustbins full of rubbish from a citizen's home became a service he was obliged to pay for as part of his rates. At the brickworks the unwanted materials in the refuse – bottles, pot lids, broken crockery, and similar objects – were thrown onto tips after passing through the ash screens. Soon mountains of rubbish became familiar sights at most brickworks in Britain.

After 1900, when few brickworks had any use for ashes, those local corporations that depended heavily on brickworks to get rid of refuse were obliged to pay in order to continue dumping. At many brickworks there were large clay pits which their owners found they could now lease at a handsome profit to corporations for the disposal of rubbish. Needless to say, there was a further increase in rates to cover the additional cost to the corporation. It is this period in the town's history that most men in their eighties recall when they tell you that rubbish was dumped 'at the old brickworks'.

Fortunately for today's pot lid and bottle collectors these dumps are easy to find. Often an Ordnance Survey map will indicate the site of an old brickworks, especially if a chimney or one or two derelict kilns remain visible, and a search around them will soon reveal a dump. When the site is not marked on a map it can usually be found by looking for the overgrown mountains of screened rubbish that stand out from the surrounding countryside as monuments to nineteenth-century labour. When approaching the site by a cart track, if the refuse was carted, or a canal bank if it came by barge, the old tips will be among the first things you see.

Most nineteenth-century brickmaking sites will be derelict. Deposits of clay ran out years ago, but a few still operate as factories turning out concrete paving stones or ornamental walling blocks. In such a case the original brickworks site may be some distance from the modern buildings. Its exact location can be pin-pointed by poking around in the undergrowth for fallen walls and the foundations of kilns and other buildings. Occasionally the screening machinery used in the nineteenth century to extract ashes is still to be seen rusting away in a forgotten corner of the site.

Vegetation on brickworks dumps

Experienced dump-diggers swap yarns about the largest nettles they have encountered in the same way that fishermen tell tales about 'the one that got away'. Invariably the dump on which the giant nettles were found will be a brickworks site. I have seen nettles eight feet tall and with leaves as big as a man's palm on brickworks' dumps; and I must warn you that their stings can be exceptionally painful. I believe they thrive so well because large amounts of unwanted refuse were burned and

this has made the soil very rich in the foods nettles require
Certainly the largest nettles are always to be found where ther
is evidence that the dump was once alight. Elders and bramble
grow equally well.

I am confident that every beginner at dump-hunting wh
can find within himself the patience to carry out his searche
as outlined above will locate his first Victorian or Edwardia
refuse site within a few days of buying this book. Failure t
find a dump at the first, second or even third attempt mus
not be accepted as total failure at the hobby. Something i
learned even from abortive expeditions because they eliminat
certain areas of land from the search and thereby increase th
chances of success next time. They also teach you to look care
fully at the ground you are walking over and greatly improv
your knowledge of local topography. The secret of success i
not only to apply the rules set out above; it is also to kee
on applying them when the less determined have given up. I
you can do that you will soon be rewarded with the findin
of your first pot lid.

Dump-finder's chart

Type of dump	Possible location	Visible clues	Vegetation
Clay, sand, gravel, or chalk pit	Wherever these materials were formerly excavated	Cart tracks, glass or pottery fragments on ploughed fields or in roots of vegetation	Elders, nettles, brambles
Land reclamation sites	Former marshland on river estuaries or the coast	Embankments, sea walls, derelict staithes in dried-out creeks	Dry reed thistles
Derelict brickworks	Wherever good brick-making clay could be obtained	Chimneys, derelict kilns, high mounds of overgrown refuse	Giant nettles, elders, brambles,
Canalside dumps	On all canal routes	Derelict barge moorings	Elders, nettles, brambles
House and farm dumps	In gardens or on sloping ground at the rear of large Victorian farms and houses	Footpaths or tracks leading from house to dump	Nettles

Small dumps

There are a few towns in Britain where large Victorian o
Edwardian dumps cannot be found because the towns did no
exist in those days. Readers who live in them must conten
themselves with much smaller dumps on large farms or nea
old houses in the surrounding countryside. Although insignifi-
cant in volume when compared with town dumps, these sites
often contain very interesting finds and, because their Victoria
occupants were usually quite rich, a fair selection of pot lids.
The dumps are almost always situated at the rear of a house;

occasionally in the garden, more often at the bottom of an overgrown or wooded slope where rubbish could be dumped without spoiling the scenery or occupying land suitable for growing crops. A track or pathway leading from the kitchen door to the dump can sometimes be seen. Nettles grow profusely on top of the refuse.

Permission for a dig

Having found your first local site you must now find the owner of the land on which the dump is situated. This is often the most difficult problem a digger has to face and one which gives headaches to beginners and experienced pot lid hunters alike. The difficulty lies in the fact that many dumps are situated on derelict land owned by absentee landlords whose business addresses can be many miles from the site a digger hopes to work on. The only means of contact is by letter and it is usually the devil's own job to locate the person within the organization who handles such obscure problems as giving permission for dump-digging activities. I can give some idea of the tangled web of dump ownership by recalling one or two of my own experiences when trying to obtain permission to dig sites.

Several years ago I located an interesting dump on derelict land in Essex. It was a huge site and part of it was being used by a local timber company as a storage area for unsawn logs. I talked to a foreman working nearby who informed me the land was owned by the timber company and, after obtaining the name of the company secretary from him, I went home and wrote a letter to this gentleman requesting permission to dig. The company secretary's reply explained that his firm merely leased the site and could not give permission for my dig. He did, however, provide the address of the owners and I wrote a second letter to them. The reply I received came from an entirely different company then occupying the address I wrote to; it stated that the other firm was in liquidation and that its affairs were being handled by a firm of solicitors in London. Off went my third letter to the solicitors and when the reply came I opened the envelope with some apprehension. Happily, the reply was most friendly. Not only was permission given, but one of the partners in the firm was himself a keen bottle collector and most anxious to join me on the dig!

On another occasion I approached a farmer with a verbal request to dig a site and I received a blunt refusal because, he said, several diggers had already been caught on the site excavating without his permission. He was somewhat mollified when I told him I deplored such behaviour and offered to clean up the mess the unwelcome diggers had made, but he would not change his mind. There matters rested for several months until I learned, quite by chance, that the strip of land on which the dump was situated actually belonged to a property developing company; the farm boundary ran alongside the site but it did not take in the dump. When I wrote to the company they agreed at once to let me dig, on condition that the farmer allowed access to the site across his land. After two further meetings with the farmer, during which I was able to convince him of my genuine interest in nineteenth-century container history and of my ability to dig the site methodically and neatly, I was eventually able to obtain the required permission for access. I dug up my first pot lid eleven months after finding the dump.

Every dump-digger can recount similar stories and each has learned that difficulties encountered when trying to obtain permission for a dig can usually be overcome by persistence when tracking down site owners and politeness when writing or talking to them. A face-to-face meeting with the landowner is usually more successful than approaches by letter or telephone. I recommend it when seeking permission from farmers and landowners who live close to a site because most people are better at friendly conversations than they are at writing rather formal letters. When meeting a landowner for the first time you should, if possible, take with you one or two objects recovered from other nineteenth-century dumps because it is most unlikely that a landowner who takes no interest in the hobby will have any idea what pot lids or Codd's bottles are. If you have yet to make a dump find you might profitably take a copy of this book with you and show the landowner the photographs it contains.

It is most important that you impress on the landowner your genuine enthusiasm for the hobby. If you appear to possess little more than a half-hearted interest in poking around his land he will not feel he is depriving you of much pleasure by refusing your request. Explain that although the dump might seem to him nothing more than a nettle-covered and unproductive piece of ground, to you it is a mine of information on local history and that by recovering objects from it you will add to everyone's knowledge of Victorian society.

It is even more important that you assure him you will not make a mess when digging the site. Almost all refusals are given because owners imagine sites will be left looking like battlefields when the dig is completed and their dumps will be transformed from untidy but not unpleasant patches of weeds to bomb craters strewn with broken glass. Point out that methodical excavation of the site requires the digging of neat trenches which are always filled in when the excavation is finished; and give your word that the site will be cleaned up to his satisfaction on completion of the dig. It is also worth mentioning that all digging is done with hand tools and not with bulldozers or mechanical shovels as some landowners imagine when one talks of 'digging' a site.

Another point worth mentioning during your conversation is that the landowner or any members of his family who might like to join in the dig would be made welcome. Most will smile and shake their heads at this suggestion when it is first made, but many change their minds when they see some of the objects you recover. I have known landowners progress from total disinterest to active enthusiasm after one look in a trench I have dug on their dumps.

Few landowners will refuse to allow you to dig if these three main points are stressed during your meeting, though many will insist on making conditions about the number of people who visit the site and the times when you will be allowed to carry out the work. Some farmers prefer visitors during winter months when they are least likely to disrupt farm work; others will insist that you dig only at weekends or on certain days of the week. Whatever the conditions the landowner makes you *must* accept them and keep to them during the entire digging period. You must also accept your share of blunt refusals. All diggers meet with them from time to time and there is nothing that can be done if the man who owns a dump says you cannot dig it. If your initial investigation of the site suggested it might be rich in pot lids it is sometimes worth writing to the landowner a few weeks after your meeting in the hope that he might have a change of heart. At the very least your letter will remind him of your name and address should he decide to allow a dig in the future.

Occasionally you will find a site owned by an absentee landlord with a large signboard erected on it which usually begins 'this site acquired for development by...'. This should not be taken to mean that a factory or office block is about to be built; many sites remain desolate for years, often until their signboards rot away with age. Make a note of the developer's address and when you get home write a letter to the company secretary on the following lines:

Dear Sir,

I write in connection with a plot of land at (give accurate location) which is owned by your company and on which you plan a future development. On the site is an old refuse dump which I have dated by research to the late Victorian period. I take an enthusiastic interest in local history and I would like to carry out a small excavation of the dump before the site is developed in order to recover some of the nineteenth-century bottles and other containers buried there.

This letter is to ask if you will grant permission for the excavation which involves the hand-digging of a trench approximately ten yards long by one yard wide to a depth of three or four feet. The work would be carried out at weekends during a period of one month. I will, of course, refill the trench on completion of the dig and take great ware to leave the site exactly as found.

Your permission for this project will help increase knowledge of Victorian social history and give to me the pleasure and satisfaction of excavating a most interesting nineteenth-century dump. I look forward to your reply for which I enclose an addressed and pre-paid envelope.

Yours faithfully,

I offer no guarantee that such a letter will bring approval for your dig, but your hopes might be raised by knowing that

I have written similar letters to many companies during my years of interest in the hobby and I am not disappointed with my success rate. The most likely reason for a refusal will be that the developers intend to commence work on the site in the immediate future. If that is the case it is worth writing again to the company secretary to ask if you might be allowed to visit the site when trenches are dug for water, gas, electricity and other services; many good finds can be made by checking spoil heaps left by mechanical diggers when they cut through a dump.

Most sites have no signboards to indicate ownership; unless you can obtain information from a local farmhouse or from someone working nearby you will have to call at your town hall in order to trace the landowner. Visit the planning department where the landowner's name and address should be recorded. The clerk in the office will require an accurate location of the site in order to trace ownership; take with you the Ordnance Survey map on which you have marked the dump's position. Addresses provided are often those of parent companies who have delegated responsibility for developing sites to subsidiaries, but if you write to the company secretary of the parent company he will either forward your letter to the subsidiary or reply giving you another address to write to. Be prepared to write several letters before you eventually make contact with the right man.

Finally, I urge you to keep copies of all correspondence with landowners on the subject of permission for digs. In time you will own an impressive file of letters which, if shown to local farmers and landowners when requesting permission for future digs, will help to convince them of your ability to carry out the work to their satisfaction.

Digging tools and digging methods

With the dump located and permission to dig it obtained, work can now begin on recovering some of the pot lids you hope it will contain. The tools and equipment required for this job are:

> a strong garden fork
> a wide shovel with a fairly long handle
> a steel probe rod five feet long and at least half an inch
>   thick with a short handle at one end
> four wooden pegs twelve inches long
> twenty yards of string
> an ex-Army kitbag with shoulder strap
> an old pair of gloves
> a dozen old newspapers

Most experienced diggers intent on digging one site for a period of weeks or months hide their tools and equipment somewhere near the site when each day's dig comes to an end. This saves the effort of carrying tools back and forth to the site and

gives extra room in the kitbag for finds. It is a useful tip, but its success depends on well-hidden tools.

Confirming age of dump

Your first task is to dig a short trial trench to confirm the dump's age and the depth of refuse. Select a spot on which the vegetation is thickest and clear nettles and grass from an area five square yards around it. This is done best with the fork which can also be used to rake the vegetation to one side of the cleared area. Next stake out two parallel lines one yard apart across the cleared area with your pegs and string. Loosen up the topsoil between the lines with your fork and shovel it out on *one side* of the trench. Loosen more earth and shovel once again, making quite sure you keep the walls of your trench vertical and that you remove earth in such a way that the bottom of the trench remains level. When you reach a depth of two or three feet you should notice a change in the composition of the material you are digging out. The brownish, clayey soil found in the top covering should now give way to grey or black

The author at work. A trench sufficiently wide for comfortable working has been cut. Sides are kept vertical and spoil is thrown on one side only. Note dead, winter vegetation at top of picture. In summer nettles grow several feet tall here.

Broken fragments you should find near the surface if the dump is of the correct age to contain pot lids.

material composed largely of ashes mixed with fragments of glass, pottery and other man-made objects. When the mound of earth you are throwing up along one side of the trench has a generous covering of these fragments take a rest from your digging to examine them closely. In a dump likely to contain pot lids the fragments visible on the mound *must* include some or all of the following items:

> clay tobacco pipe stems
> necks from broken Codd's bottles
> other pieces of green bottle glass
> glass marbles
> heads or limbs from miniature china dolls
> broken bases (or lids) from earthenware pots

If the material on your spoil heap contains none of these it is most unlikely that further digging will reveal pot lids. The dump probably dates from a period after 1920. Check the mound carefully once again to see if you can find any of the following:

> bottle necks with external screw threads
> metal bottle caps
> colourless bottle glass
> any objects made from plastic or bakelite
> brass caps from broken light bulbs
> pieces of rubber

If you have dug out any of these I am prepared to bet a bear's grease lid that your dump is much too modern to contain even plain pot lids. Fill in the trial trench and start looking for your second dump.

Broken pipe stems are the commonest finds in the top two or three feet of a dump likely to contain pot lids. The fragments will be one or two inches long and light grey, brown, or orange in colour. The more you find the greater are the chances that pot lids lie beneath your feet. If most of the stems are less than a quarter of an inch thick and some have raised designs or decorations on them I am prepared to bet another bear's grease lid that you will find your first pot lid within the next few hours. Thin, decorated stems were used on pipes made before 1900; they were made much thicker and without decoration from then until 1910 by which time cigarette smoking had almost killed off the pipe-making industry.

Necks from Codd's bottles are not always an indication that a dump is of great age because these bottles were used in some districts up to 1920; but when they are found together with fragments of bottles made from green or aqua-coloured glass they suggest at least an Edwardian and possibly a Victorian site. The dump is almost certainly Victorian if you find pieces of green glass from round-bottomed, or Hamilton bottles. Again, these bottles take their name from the inventor, William Hamilton, and they were used for mineral waters throughout the Victorian period.

There are many diggers who hunt for nothing else but dolls' heads. If they chance to find transfer-printed pot lid fragments when they cut a trial trench on a new site they know that dolls' heads are sure to turn up. If the heads you find are very small – less than one inch in diameter – your dump is sure to hold pot lids. Some larger heads up to two inches in diameter are found in later dumps, but even these sites are old enough to contain transfer-printed earthenware.

Having found some or all of these items in the material already removed, take the probe rod and thrust it into the bottom of the trench. It will cut through cindery dump material as readily as a hot knife cuts butter, and by probing the trench floor you can confirm the depth of refuse beneath it. If the shaft goes in easily this means there is a good seam of refuse that might hold pot lids; but if the rod strikes clay almost at once over the entire area of the floor the dump is either very shallow or it was capped with clay before dumping ceased altogether. Experienced diggers will know that it is sometimes possible to dig through a cap of clay to the refuse buried beneath, but this involves strenuous and very deep digging and is not recommended to beginners. Before abandoning a site that seems too shallow to contain anything but broken objects, wander around with your probe rod and attempt to find a deeper seam of refuse. If you draw a plan of the site and mark your probing spots on it you can define the perimeter of the dump in this way. You can also work out the most productive line for your trench and on which side of it spoil should be thrown so that the refuse is not even more deeply buried.

Quite often when a trench five yards in length is cut across a dump, part of it will reach the solid walls of the original hole. If this occurs, extend the trench so that you have a five-yard stretch of refuse to explore. Remember to keep the extension as wide as the original trench and ensure the walls are vertical before you explore deeper material. Complete bottles, clay tobacco pipes, and, hopefully, pot lids can be expected to reveal themselves now. Dig carefully *with the fork only*. Push the tines deep into the cindery earth and pull the handle backwards to loosen it. Complete objects will be trapped on the tines and be easy to spot if you keep your eyes on the job. Lift them out by hand and place them on the opposite side of the trench to that on which you are throwing the spoil.

Most beginners reach this stage of the dig without mishap but the majority proceed to make the fatal mistake of raking the walls of the trench and of digging deeply into the floor in one spot. The results are falling trench walls and an uneven floor on which to stand while digging. Within half an hour the neatly cut trench becomes a cone-shaped hole with unstable walls that keep falling in. The digger spends most of the remainder of the day trying to keep the depth of the hole at three feet and the few finds he does make come from an even shallower depth. As is explained in the following chapter, most of the objects in the top two or three feet of a dump are broken – hence the poor recovery rate of most beginners.

The remedy is simple: Make a determined effort to resist the temptation to poke the walls of the trench and keep the floor level by working back and forth across the trench when loosening material with the fork and throwing out the spoil. Continue downwards in this way, pausing now and again to examine the ground before you dig it, on the lookout for pot lids with their edges partly revealed. Work at a steady, methodical pace; you are not attempting to break the world record as a muck shifter. It is far more profitable in pot lid finds to dig a trench four feet deep from which every lid has been recovered than it is to exhaust yourself digging to six feet by working too quickly and probably throwing lids out on to the spoil heap.

When you reach a depth at which it becomes difficult to throw out shovelfuls of earth you should not go deeper. Climb out of the trench by walking to one end so that you do not loosen the walls or cause the spoil heap to fall in. Pick up your finds and wrap each in a sheet of newspaper before placing them in your kitbag. Now move the pegs and string on that side of the trench half a yard back from the edge. This is the line you must keep to during the next stage of the dig. Remove the topsoil to a depth of two feet and throw it across the trench on to the spoil heap. Climb back into the trench and begin to rake the material in this stepped wall across to the other

A common mistake made by beginners is to dig a trench which is too narrow for comfortable work.

The walls must be cut back with the fork to provide sufficient room for comfortable digging.

Raking the trench walls like this causes the trench to lose depth. Dig *downwards*, not sideways.

When visiting sites that have been incorrectly excavated by other diggers, try raking beneath tree roots which have not been fully explored.

A nice pot lid find. The previous digger missed it by inches because he used incorrect digging techniques.

side of the trench, keeping your eyes open for pot lids. The material is moved across the trench by a combination of raking with the fork and compacting with the back of the shovel; the end result should be a stepped wall on the spoil heap side of the trench, and a clean, vertical wall on the other, while the floor should remain at the depth to which you first dug.

When you move your pegs and string to take in the next half-yard section you can throw some of the clayey topsoil onto the stepped wall to bring it level with the spoil heap. By using this step-digging method – the only successful way to dig a dump – it is possible to excavate the entire site to a reasonable depth with only one continuously moving trench. When the excavation is completed the spoil taken from the first trench is used to fill in the last one and the site is left neat and tidy.

Within a month nettles will colonize the newly exposed soil; within two there will be nothing to suggest it was ever disturbed - apart from your collection of pot lids.

Documentary research

Lengthy discussions with many diggers have convinced me that beginners generally achieve a greater dump-finding success rate when they use the 'talk-and-walk' method already described than they do by spending hours sifting through nineteenth-century documents at town halls and public libraries. Nevertheless, the latter method of locating sites is used in combination with the 'talk-and-walk' method by most experienced diggers and it does, therefore, merit a paragraph or two here. It involves little more than sitting in the reference department of your local public library reading Victorian Corporation Minutes in the hope of finding written information relating to refuse collection and disposal. Most of the clues found will be Corporation Engineer's reports on the number of tons of refuse collected from households in the town, the leasing of dumping sites, or complaints from residents living near a dump about its offensive smell. It all makes fascinating reading and it certainly can suggest areas that might be profitably searched for Victorian dumps.

I was given an ideal opportunity to demonstrate the method used in, and the results achieved by, documentary research quite recently when I moved house and left 'those dumps I know so well' around London to live in York, a city I had not set foot in before. It has an excellent reference library, well endowed with local records which I have not yet had time to delve deeply into; but I did have a brief look at nineteenth-century Corporation Minutes kept on the shelves and in half an hour was rewarded with three possible leads to worthwhile dumps:

1. A report, dated 1899, that one City Councillor had urged that dumping of refuse near the site of a sewage works should cease, presumably because of the high cost of carting refuse to the spot;

2. A report in the same year that the Corporation Engineer had leased an area 'of low-lying land adjoining tan pits' at the rear of a tannery for the dumping of household refuse at a cost of two and a half pence per waggonload;

3. A complaint made in 1902 by residents in a street close to another dump about the offensive smell of rubbish dumped there.

Inspection of a modern map of the city showed that although none of the sites had been built on, the dump near the sewage works had been landscaped to provide a riverside walk, and the dump which had offended people with its smell had later formed the foundation for a football pitch. The tannery site

The old tannery site at York.

Elders growing near the tan pits. A single bottle can be seen poking out from the roots of the tree nearest the camera.

seemed undisturbed so I took a morning off from labouring over my typewriter and went to have a look at the spot. The tannery, a fine Victorian building, was now in use as a storage depot, having ceased operations 'before the War' I was informed by an old gentleman of sixty I met in the district. He had no idea where the tan pits had been situated but I found them by poking in the undergrowth behind the building. There was a steep slope at the side of the pits that ran down to what had been the 'low-lying land', but which was now partially levelled by the dumping of modern brick rubble. The sides of the slope were covered with a tangle of vegetation including several elders, and when I looked around their roots I could see large amounts of broken glass and pottery. Some of the glass fragments were obviously from Codd's bottles and further poking produced a single glass marble. Apparently some of the refuse tipped down the slope had lodged there in sufficient quantities to encourage the growth of the dump-loving trees.

There the matter has rested since that day (though I have now traced the landowner) because shortly afterwards I became involved with a far more exciting pot lid dump at Harrogate; but I hope to dig my first dump in York a few weeks from now.

Experienced diggers who plan searches around the towns mentioned earlier as likely to have dumps with large numbers of pot lids will, I am sure, make full use of public libraries, newspaper offices and town halls. They will also talk to as many old residents as they can meet and tramp miles into the surrounding countryside to check on possible sites. It is quite unnecessary for me to give them detailed advice on research, search and digging techniques; they have each learned such things well during years of interest in the hobby. Their techniques are in fact those already explained in this chapter, the only difference being that experienced dump-hunters ask more questions of old people, read official records more thoroughly, look at the ground

David Lewis of Harrogate explores a local dump.

Above and opposite:
Some of the northern lids found by David Lewis when he excavated a Harrogate dump.

they are walking over more closely, and dig rather deeper than newcomers to the game. That is why they have large collection of pot lids.

I dearly wish I could accompany each and every one of them around the sites I have suggested and listen to the whoops of delight when they unearth the rare black and whites and unrecorded coloured specimens which *are* going to be found during the next few years. I recently had a foretaste of what is in store when I visited Harrogate shortly after coming to live in the north. Through the British Bottle Collectors' Club I made contact with David Lewis, at that time the only club member living in Harrogate. As David will agree, he was an inexperienced dump-digger when we met; he had been a club member

for only a few months and the limited digging he had done had been on sites in other areas.

During our first meeting I whetted his appetite for home-town dumps by telling him that in 1889 there were no less than twelve chemist's shops in Harrogate and five in neighbouring Knaresborough, and that I was convinced the town's dumps held large numbers of lids. Within a few days David proved my theory; he found his first Harrogate dump and started his collection of transfer-printed pot lids. At the present time, only a couple of weeks after our first meeting, his collection amounts to thirty-five and includes lids from Harrogate, Glasgow, Sheffield and London. On one well-remembered day he found ten lids in a couple of hours!

4 Cleaning, repairs and display

Many of the lids dug out of Victorian refuse sites require nothing more than a wash in warm, soapy water to restore them to their original condition. These specimens are highly prized by diggers and eagerly sought by non-digging collectors who pay top prices for them because of their perfect condition and because they will surely increase in value as more and more people take an interest in pot lid collecting.

A second and much larger group of dump-found lids are discoloured and stained when first dug out of the ground. They are most often found in dumps which have been burned at some time in the past, or which contain large amounts of rusted iron. Slight burning causes the white areas of a transfer to discolour to grey; severe burning destroys the transfer completely because the glaze protecting it is melted by the fire and the ink beneath is scorched by the heat. Nothing can be done to save these badly burned lids, but many of the discoloured specimens can be restored by removing or lightening the greyness in the transfer.

Bleaching

This is done by bleaching the lids in chemicals of varying strengths. Success depends on proceeding *slowly* from weak to strong chemicals and on allowing the weaker solutions sufficient time to act upon the discolouration before trying something stronger. Impatient attempts to speed the bleaching by plunging lids into powerful acids usually results in making the lids look even more unsightly. It is much safer to allow a lid to soak for ten days in a mild bleach than it is to give it two minutes in undiluted acid.

The containers for the bleaching solutions should be glazed earthenware pudding basins specially bought for the job. *Do not borrow them from the kitchen and use them again for food when cleaning is completed.* If you plan to dig regularly you will always need cleaning materials and the solutions can be used many times before being discarded. Experienced diggers keep a lookout for suitable bowls and basins when digging their dumps.

I must remind you before proceeding that most chemicals

A rare and beautiful lid badly stained by burning. The fire melted the glaze. Any attempt to clean the lid with acids would cause further damage to the transfer.

used for cleaning pot lids, bottles and other dump finds are poisons – *highly dangerous to children.* If you cannot keep basins for the solutions in a locked garage or shed and well out of reach of small hands they should be emptied down an outside sink when each operation is completed. It is also extremely dangerous to mix chemicals together. Do not try to produce a 'magic whitening brew' by stirring all the household cleaners you can find into one basin. You will produce a choking gas if you do so.

The following solutions should be made up, one to each basin, for bleaching operations:

1. A strong solution of washing soda made by half filling the basin with boiling water and dissolving in it as much soda as possible;
2. A solution made by dissolving as much powdered lavatory cleaner as possible in a basin half filled with warm water;
3. A basin half filled with undiluted 'Domestos';
4. A basin half filled with a solution made by adding one part concentrated hydrochloric acid to four parts rainwater. (The acid can be obtained from builders' merchants. Obtain the rainwater by standing a bucket in the garden on a rainy day.) Rubber gloves should be worn when handling acid, and when carrying out the cleaning operations described in this chapter.

The basins should hold half a dozen lids. It is therefore a time-saving plan to delay cleaning operations until you have found or purchased six discoloured lids. They should first be washed thoroughly in warm, soapy water and scrubbed with an old toothbrush to remove dirt from back and front. If you use a plastic washing up bowl for this operation and wash one lid at a time you reduce the risk of accidental damage caused by dropping a lid from soapy hands. When the six lids are clean examine them carefully and decide which are slightly discoloured and which will require more thorough bleaching. The slightly discoloured ones must go into the washing soda, the others into solution no. 2.

After twenty-four hours take out each lid and confirm that there has been some improvement in its colour. If it is slightly whiter than it was the day before but still obviously discoloured return it to the same basin. If it is fully whitened it can be washed thoroughly in running water to remove all traces of chemicals before it is added to your collection. If there has been no improvement in its colour the bleach in which you soaked it was too weak. Place it in the next strongest solution for another twenty-four hours. Thus a lid unaffected by its overnight soak in washing soda is now placed in the lavatory cleaner and one which has not been improved by that solution goes into the undiluted 'Domestos'. This progression continues for several days. Whenever a lid fails to improve during a twenty-four hour period and is not yet fully whitened it goes into the next strongest solution. Every lid reaching the acid stage must be inspected at twelve-hourly intervals and bleaching must stop immediately there is no improvement in the colour of the lid – even though it is not yet fully white. I do not recommend further attempts to remove the discolouration by soaking in even stronger acids. Accept the lid with its imperfections rather than risk harm to the glaze or transfer by drastic attempts at cleaning.

Removing iron stains
Lids that cannot be fully whitened by bleaching are not unattractive when displayed alongside white lids, but lids with brown iron stains across their surfaces look unsightly whether the lids are white or grey. To remove iron stains you will require the acid solution used in the bleaching process and another basin containing rainwater. First remove as much of the stain as possible by washing the lid in warm, soapy water. In addition to the toothbrush used to get rid of dirt you should also use a *plastic* scouring pad on the stained area. (Metal scouring pads must not be used. They will scratch the glaze on the lid.) Rub vigorously using plenty of soap and most iron stains will be completely removed. Others must be treated by soaking the lids for twelve hours in the acid solution after which the stains are rubbed once again with the scouring pad in warm, soapy water. The lids are then thoroughly rinsed to remove all traces of soap and placed in the rainwater for another twelve hours.

This final soaking in rainwater is most important. If it is left out of the process lids that were iron-stained will begin to turn yellow after a few days as tiny amounts of acid remaining in the cracks on the glaze react with microscopic particles of rust not washed from the lid. Tap water is unsuitable because it contains chlorine which reacts with the acid to add to the

iscolouration. Some lids treated with acid to remove fire disco-
ouration also begin to turn yellow several days after cleaning
completed. The yellowness is removed by placing the lids
rainwater for a few hours and then drying them thoroughly
n a clean cloth. Repeat the process if the yellow discolouration
eturns.

Many iron-stained and fire-discoloured lids can be restored
perfect condition by careful cleaning after which they become
valuable as lids found without imperfections. Those not fully
estored can be added to your collection until you dig or obtain
perfect specimen.

Other stains

Oils and chemicals of all kinds occasionally stain lids in refuse
umps and it is impossible to prescribe a single treatment to
emove the stains, because a remedy successful on one lid will
o nothing to improve the appearance of another. Each must
e treated as an individual case on which a variety of treatments
none of them drastic – are tried until the stain is removed
r reduced to an acceptable level. Treatments I know to have
een tried with success on lids stained by oils and chemicals
nclude:

Soap and warm water	Long periods of soaking and scrubbing with a plastic scourer recommended.
Carbon tetrachloride	Excellent on oil and tar stains. Use with care and follow manufacturer's instructions regarding ventilation.
Baking	This method is used on oil stains that have penetrated beneath the glaze. The lid is placed in a gas oven which is brought *slowly* to maximum heat and the lid is baked for ten minutes. It is then removed while still hot and rubbed vigorously with a dry cloth which soaks up the oil. Repeat several times.
Boiling	The lid is placed in a pan of cold water which is brought *slowly* to boiling point and allowed to simmer for an hour or two. Allow the water to cool slowly before removing the lid.

Repairing chips and breaks

Broken and chipped lids can be bought very cheaply from dig-
ers and dealers by collectors unable to dig their own dumps
nd who cannot afford to buy perfect specimens. Although
epaired lids are never likely to become valuable collectors' items
hey bring the pleasures and satisfactions of pot lid ownership
o many people who might otherwise be without a modest col-
ection. I know of one or two repairers who have developed
uch a high degree of skill it is almost impossible to distinguish
etween their repaired lids and perfect specimens. The standard

of the few repairs I have attempted falls far short of this becaus
I am a digger by inclination; but the materials and method
used by these experts are the same as those described her
Any reader with a flair for this type of work should in tim
be able to repair damaged lids to a high professional standard

It is not difficult to find all the pieces of a broken lid i
a rubbish dump because most of the breakages occur in th
dump and not, as might be expected, during tipping. Pot lid
are remarkably tough; they can withstand deep burial, moderat
burning, and most knocks apart from a direct blow with a dig
ging fork. As all experienced diggers know it is uncommon t
find broken specimens at depths beyond three feet because i
is the freezing and melting of rainwater in the top two or thre
feet of the dump during winter that breaks most lids. The wate
which does not seep down beyond three feet, gets into minut
cracks where it freezes and expands to widen them and even
tually break the lid. Most diggers do not bother to keep thes
broken pieces unless the find is a rare lid, but if you let i
be known you are interested in them you will be able to bu
the pieces very cheaply. They are repaired by gluing with
clear, waterproof adhesive suitable for repairing china. If frag
ments are missing they can be replaced using the method no
described for repairing chipped lids.

The two main causes of chipped lids are freezing water an
incorrect digging techniques. If the glaze on a lid become
crazed when a dump is burned, water can find its way int
the minute cracks on the surface where it freezes in winter an
causes parts of the lid to break away, often leaving a bare patc
on an otherwise complete lid. Similar damage is caused whe
a digging fork is thrust into a dump with too much force an
one of its tines strikes the lid a glancing blow. Whatever th
cause, the result is an imperfect lid; to repair it the followin
are required:

'Sylmasta' ceramic putty	This is a non-shrinking, epoxy resi material which can be hardened in a fe minutes. When hard its appearance i similar to earthenware. Sold in hard ware stores.
Drawing pens	A selection of extra-fine nibs ar required for inking-in missing areas c the damaged transfer. Sold by drawin office equipment suppliers.
Transparent varnish	This is used to simulate glaze on th repaired area of a lid. Polyurethene var nish in a spray can is suitable; also th varnishes sold in artists' materials shop for use on clay models.
Also	Indian ink; small amounts of black an white powder paints; small artist's pain brush; soft cloth; washing up liquid.

The broken pieces of this lid were recovered from the upper layers of a Victorian dump.

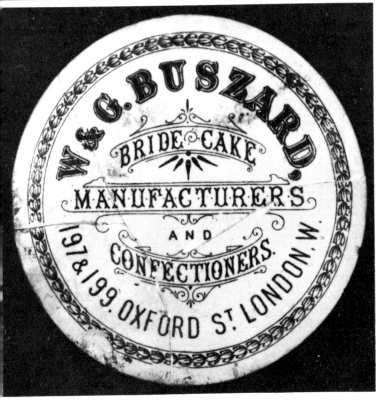

When glued together using clear, waterproof glue, these pieces make a lid worth keeping, although it will not be valuable.

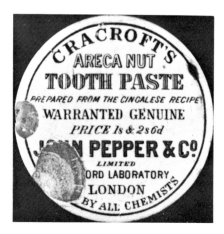 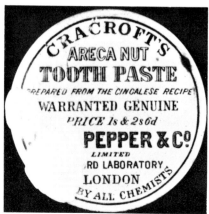 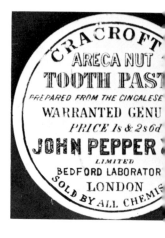

Stages in repairing a lid damaged by freezing water. The missing areas of the lid are filled with 'Sylmasta' and the putty smoothed before hardening in the oven. Indian ink is then used to add letters and border missing from the transfer.

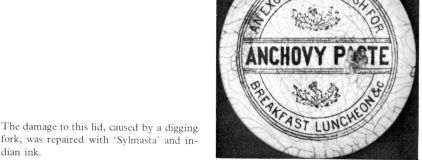 

The damage to this lid, caused by a digging fork, was repaired with 'Sylmasta' and indian ink.

Any discolouration or stains on the undamaged areas of the lid must be treated before repairs begin. After treatment the lid is thoroughly dried by placing it on a radiator or close to a fire for a day or two. It is of the utmost importance that damaged areas are thoroughly dry before the repair work begins.

The ceramic putty is supplied in two tins, equal amounts being taken from each and thoroughly kneaded together. The colour of the material at this stage is a very close match to the white areas of most pot lids, but if it is too light or too dark for your lid you should mix in tiny amounts of black or white powder paint until the correct colour is achieved. The putty is now pressed into the chipped area and smoothed by wiping it with a soft cloth previously dipped in washing-up liquid. The cloth removes excess putty around the chip so that the area filled in matches the contours of the lid perfectly.

The repair is hardened by placing the lid in a warm oven for fifteen to twenty minutes after which time the putty will be like stone. Missing areas of black lettering or decoration can be carefully drawn on it with indian ink which is left to dry before the varnish is applied to the putty in order to match the glaze on the remainder of the lid. Similar techniques are used to repair wide cracks in lids which have been glued together from broken pieces.

Displaying pot lids

It is possible to buy round frames and small plate hangers at some antique shops or through advertisements in antiques magazines. They are used to display pot lids on walls, but the frames are quite expensive and the rather unattractive wire hangers, which can be seen when the lids are hung, mar the appearance of the display. Readers with woodworking skills will be able to make their own attractive frames; the less skilful who do not wish to spend too much on display materials will find the following method of displaying their lids most useful.

A piece of thick hardboard twenty-four inches long and sixteen inches wide is primed and given a coat of blackboard paint. Pieces of suitably decorated wood, one inch wide, are glued around the edges to form a false frame and a hanging cord is fixed at the back of the hardboard. A dozen lids can now be set out on the hardboard and, when a satisfactory arrangement has been decided upon, they can be glued with an adhesive (such as 'Bostik') suitable for joining china to wood. When the glue has hardened the display is ready for hanging.

The disadvantage of this method is, of course, that lids cannot easily be removed once they have been glued to the board; but this is not a great disadvantage if the lids are to form a permanent collection. Readers who wish to handle their lids regularly, to exchange them, or to take them to exhibitions will find it more convenient to display their collection by setting out the lids on a flat shelf. The appearance of such a display is greatly improved if some of the lids are placed on matching bases which can be found on any dump.

5 Buying, selling and exchanging

Joining a club

Every collector who obtains his pot lids by digging Victorian and Edwardian rubbish dumps should join the British Bottle Collectors' Club. Although membership is not essential for non-digging collectors, there are a number of benefits to be gained from membership by anyone whose interest in lids extends to buying, selling and exchanges. The club was formed several years ago by a handful of bottle collectors in London who decided to pool their knowledge of sites and their historical information on the bottles they had recovered from them. Most of the dumps being excavated at that time were in Essex and Kent and within a few months the club had detailed information on all known Victorian and Edwardian refuse sites in the two counties together with comprehensive files listing all the bottles found in them. Each member was given the task of obtaining additional information on the brewers, mineral water makers, and chemists' shops in business in the member's home town during the late nineteenth and early twentieth centuries. This was added to the cards in the club's files with photographs and drawings of the bottles used by these companies and found by the diggers.

By 1972 the club had members in most counties in Britain and the information stored in its files had been extended to include clay tobacco pipe and pot lid finds. The files were soon so bulky that it became inconvenient to store them at the club's headquarters; to overcome this problem and to make the information in the files more accessible to members living in other parts of the country, local club secretaries were appointed in each county and given those files relating to bottles, pipes and pot lids made or found in their counties. Local members were then asked to pass on additional information they obtained on their finds to their own county secretary.

Club membership had now reached several thousands and many of those joining were absolute beginners at the hobby. To help these newcomers it was decided the club would in future hold group digs on sites found by more experienced members on which all members within a county could benefit from the experience of a properly organized excavation. Permis-

ion to carry out these activities was obtained from many landowners, including several town councils aware of growing interest in local Victorian history. Today these group digs are
extremely popular and often attended by hundreds of diggers.

Equally well attended are the swap meetings, now held regularly in most counties, at which members exchange their duplicate bottles, pipes and pot lids. The meetings usually take place
once every two months and are held at a member's home or
a local pub. Some, notably those held by the club's London
branch, attract members from all parts of Britain. Hundreds
of deals, trades and transactions take place between members
and there is much friendly bidding and bargaining as the value
of one find is weighed against another. When the find-swapping
is completed many diggers go on to make arrangements to dig
each other's sites. One member will invite another to his private
site for a day in exchange for a return visit to the other's site
at a later date. It is quite common to hear diggers proudly
boasting of the number of pot lids that can confidently be
expected to come to light on their sites during a day, or the
variety of bottles, pipes and pot lids their dumps contain.

The advantages of taking part in these club activities will
be obvious to all non-members, especially those who have only
recently taken up the hobby. The swap meetings offer those
who do not dig a chance to exchange their duplicate lids and
to meet many diggers from whom they will be able to obtain
lids for their collections at prices far below those charged by
antique shops. It is also possible to contact diggers in other
counties who might wish to exchange or sell lids by placing
a free advertisement in the quarterly newsletter all members
receive. In addition to members' advertisements the newsletter
names new sites on which group digs are to take place and
reports on forthcoming national events. One of these is the judg-
ing of entries in a 'best-find-of-the-year' competition. The
club's sponsor, United Glass Ltd, donates a prize of £50 to
this contest which attracts entries from every county in Britain.

The magazine *Bottles and Relics News*, which is published
by the British Bottle Collectors' Club, is another excellent
source of reasonably priced pot lids. It is read by most diggers
and dealers in dump finds and its advertising pages include
many announcements offering lids for sale. The magazine also
has illustrated pages devoted to the latest pot lid finds, and
a regular price guide that keeps diggers, dealers and collectors
up-to-date on buying and selling trends. Of more importance
to diggers are the pages devoted to factual articles on bottle,
pipe and pot lid history, on the histories of manufacturers and
wholesalers, and on new sites recently discovered.

An increasing number of bottle shops and antique dealers
now hold regular pot lid auctions where hundreds of lids –
coloured and black and white – change hands in a single day.
Serious collectors should attend as many such auctions as possible, whether or not they take part in the bidding. By following

the proceedings closely a collector soon learns to recognize those lids most sought after by other collectors, and what they are prepared to pay to obtain them. He also begins to appreciate to what extent the condition of a lid affects its value and why he should always examine any lid very closely for cracks, chips and stains before offering a price close to its current value.

Reproduction lids

Readers hoping to start a collection of coloured pot lids must take extra care when buying from antique shops or bidding at auctions to ensure the lids are genuine Victorian examples and not twentieth-century reproductions worth considerably less and usually inferior in workmanship to those made in the nineteenth century. Within the last few years some coloured reproductions comparable in quality to nineteenth-century lids have been made, but most are marked on their backs to indicate they are modern in origin. It is not unknown for these marks to be erased by tricksters hoping to get a better price for their wares. If any coloured lid is offered for sale in a frame you should always insist on taking it out of the frame to examine the back before buying. If the back of the lid has been painted you would be unwise to buy it as a genuine Victorian lid.

In my opinion one of the best safeguards against being sold reproductions or fakes when buying supposed Victorian coloured pot lids is to buy from a digger and to ask him to leave any coloured lid he finds uncleaned so that you can examine it as it was when the digger found it before you decide to complete the purchase. There are no reproductions or fakes in Victorian rubbish dumps; nor can the marks of burial – minor iron stains, or slight discolouration – be convincingly added to a lid that has never been in the ground.

At the time of writing (January 1974) the British Bottle Collectors' Club has no reports of any reproduction or fake black and white lids being offered for sale. I am sure the reason for this is not that reproductions cannot be made, but that current prices for black and white lids are still far too low to make the sale of reproductions a worthwhile proposition. There are likely to be substantial increases in the values of black and white lids during the next few years as more people collect them and it seems inevitable that reproductions will appear. The British Bottle Collectors' Club has already successfully protected its members from being tricked into buying as genuine a large number of newly made Codd's bottles exported to Britain from India in 1973. The club obtained examples of these bottles and described them in detail in its newsletters so that members were able to recognize them before buying. Similar plans have been made to publicize any reproduction black and white pot lids that come on the market. They are most likely to be copies of rare bear's grease lids or others that carry high price tags. If sold as reproductions and marked as such they are harmless, but there are sure to be some people who are prepared to pass

em off as genuine Victorian lids. You should, therefore, be
utious when buying any black and white lid that shows no
gns of having been buried in a rubbish dump for a long period
especially if it is a rare example.

6 Black and white price guide

In my earlier book, *Digging up Antiques*, I included a list of approximately one hundred black and white lids most likely to be found in Victorian dumps throughout Britain. In the present volume that list has been extended to include all black and white lids found up to the time of writing by members of the British Bottle Collectors' Club. It is undoubtedly the most comprehensive list of black and white pot lids so far compiled and it makes a start on the monumental task of recording every black and white lid used in Britain during the nineteenth and early twentieth centuries.

Readers who dig up lids not recorded here should send details of their finds to the British Bottle Collectors' Club where supplementary lists will be compiled and published from time to time in the club's newsletters and in the magazine, *Bottles and Relics News*. A brief written description of each new lid is all that is required, though illustrations for the club's files will be gratefully acknowledged. Lids can be photocopied by placing them face downwards on a copying machine and holding the rubber cover on the machine tightly around them to exclude light as the copy is made. Photographers should note that good photographs of black and white lids can be made by using a copying stand. When lighting is from two 75 watt lamps and the film is rated at 50 ASA the correct exposure is one fifteenth of a second at f 11.

The alphabetical price guide used in *Digging up Antiques* is retained here. The letters A, B and C are used to indicate *approximate* retail prices for lids in perfect condition without chips, cracks or staining. The letters also provide an indication of the rarity of each lid so the differential between the categories remains constant even if inflation and demand push up prices in the future. At the present time prices in each category are

AMENDMENT
1975.
LOOSE SLIP
of PAPER
INSERTED
BETWEEN FRONT COVER.

A – £4-£6 £8 -£12
B – £6-£10 £12 -£20
C – £10-£15 £20 - £30 +

Only company names or the most important words on a lid have been used when compiling the list. Minor variations in transfers used over a long period or produced in large numbers

82

ave not been included because in some cases it would take
several hundred words to describe the variations noted by col-
ectors on lids in their possession. Thus a Wood's Areca Nut
Tooth Paste lid might have any one of six variations in the
ornamentation on its transfer while the lid might be from a
sixpenny or a shilling pot. Similarly there are at least ten known
varieties of the Atkinson's Rose Cold Cream lid. Informative
articles on transfer variations are published from time to time
in *Bottles and Relics News.*

. D. I. Tooth Powder	(B)
Allen's Lip Salve	(A)
. B. Allen's Areca Nut and Cherry Tooth Paste	(A)
Allen & Hanbury's Areca Nut Tooth Paste	(A)
Allen & Hanbury's Cherry Tooth Paste	(A)
Allen & Hanbury's Tooth Paste	(A)
American Toilet Co.'s Creme Toothpaste	(A)
American Toilet Co.'s Dr. Sheffield's Cream Dentifrice	(B)
Anchovy Paste	(A)
Angell's Dandruff Eradicator	(C)
. Anstee-Turner's Superior Cold Cream	(A)
Areca Nut Tooth Paste	(A)
Army & Navy's Areca Nut	(A)
Army & Navy's Cherry	(A)
Army & Navy Co-op's Almond Shaving Cream	(A)
Army & Navy Co-op's Cherry Tooth Paste	(A)
Army & Navy Co-op's Cold Cream of Roses	(A)
Army & Navy Co-op's Gorgona Anchovy Paste	(A)
Army & Navy Co-op's Home Made Potted Meats	(A)

Army & Navy Toilet Club's Pomade Sylphides	(C)
Army & Navy Toilet Club's United Service Shaving Cream	(B)
A. Arnold's Gipsy Ointment	(C)
Aston's Otto of Rose Cold Cream	(A)
J. Atkinson's Bear's Grease	(C)
J. Atkinson's Circassian Cream	(A)
J. Atkinson's Oriental Tooth Paste	(C)
J. Atkinson's Rose Cold Cream	(A)
J. & E. Atkinson's Glycerine Cream	(A)
J. & E. Atkinson's Naples Soap	(B)
J. & E. Atkinson's Oriental Tooth Paste	(C)
J. & E. Atkinson's Tooth Powder	(A)
Andre Autard's Creme Aspasie	(B)
B. & Co. L's Areca Nut Tooth Paste	(A)
B. & Co. L's Cherry Tooth Paste	(A)
Bailey's Perline Dentifrice	(B)
Bale's Mushroom Savoury	(B)
Ball's Superior Cold Cream	(A)

J. Barker & Co's Areca
Nut Tooth Paste (B)

Barklay & Son's Areca
Nut Tooth Paste (A)

Bayley & Co.'s Old Civet
Cat Cold Cream (B)

X. Bazin's Ambrosial
Shaving Cream (B)

Beddard's Belgravia
Tooth Paste (B)

Bedford's Sweet Honey-
suckle Tooth Paste (B)

Bell's Betel Nut Tooth
Paste (B)

Benal's Cold Cream (A)

Benbow & Sons' Areca
Nut Tooth Paste (A)

Benoist's Caviar (A)

Bensted's Pearly White
Tooth Paste (B)

H. A. Bernard – Family
Grocer (A)

R. Bird-Tench's Ant-acid
Carbolic Tooth Paste (C)

Blain's Ossepian Tooth
Powder (A)

Blanchet's Shaving
Cream (B)

Blanchflower's Bloater
Paste (C)

Blanchflower's Potted
Ham (B)

Blanchflower & Son's
Gorgona Anchovy
Paste (B)

Bleasdale's Cherry Tooth
Paste (B)

Bloater Paste (A)

Blondeau & Cie's Premier
Vinolia Shaving Soap (B)

Gustav Boehm's Anti-
Scurf Pomade (B)

Boot's Areca Nut Tooth
Paste (A)

Boot's Cherry Tooth
Paste (A)

Boot's Cold Cream (A)

Boot's Creme d'Amande (A)

Boot's Tooth Paste (A)

Boutall's Cold Cream (A)

Braddock & Bagshaw's
Diamond Eye Salve (

Bradley & Bourdas' Cold
Cream (

Bragg's Charcoal Tooth
Paste (

Brecknell Turner's Pari-
sian Shaving Cream (

Breidenbach & Co.'s
Cherry Tooth Paste (

Breidenbach & Co.'s
Amandine (

Breidenbach & Co.'s
Areca Nut Tooth Paste (

Breidenbach & Co.'s
Cherry Tooth Paste (

Breidenbach & Co.'s Cold
Cream of Roses (

Brian's Lanolin Cold
Cream (

Brighton & Hove Co-op's
Rose Cold Cream (

Bristow's Cherry Tooth
Paste (

T.F. Bristow's Shave
Easy Shaving Soap (

J. Brown's Refined Bear's
Grease (

James Brown's Clarified
Bear's Grease (

Prof. Browne's Shaving
Cream (

Buchan's Universal
Vegetable Skin Oint-
ment (

Burgess' Anchovy Paste (

Burgoyne, Burbidge's
Areca Nut Tooth Paste (

Burgoyne, Burbidge's
Cherry Tooth Paste (

Burroughs, Wellcome &
Co.'s Areca Nut Tooth
Paste (

Burroughs, Wellcome &
Co.'s Cherry Tooth
Paste (

Burroughs, Wellcome &
Co.'s Lanolin Cold
Cream (

Burroughs, Wellcome &
Co.'s Lanolin Pomade (

Burrow's Drug Stores' Dent Albo (B)

Buszard's Bride Cake (B)

C. & S. Areca Nut Tooth Paste (A)

C. & S. Cherry Tooth Paste (A)

Calvert's Carbolic Tooth Paste (A)

Carbolic Tooth Paste (A)

E. Castell Evans' Otto of Rose Cold Cream (B)

Charles' Shaving Cream (A)

Chave & Jackson's Otto of Rose Cold Cream (A)

Chavin et Cie.'s Areca Nut Tooth Paste (A)

Cherry Tooth Paste (A)

Thos. Christy & Co.'s Tooth Paste (B)

Civil Service Co-op's Areca Nut Tooth Paste (A)

Civil Service Co-op's Cherry Tooth Paste (A)

Civil Service Co-op's Cold Cream (A)

Civil Service Supply Associations's Eucalyptus and Thymol Tooth Paste (B)

Clayton's Dandelion Cocoa (C)

Cleaver's Areca Nut Tooth Paste (A)

Cleaver's Bear's Grease (B)

Cleaver's Saponaceous Tooth Paste (B)

Cleaver's Saponaceous Tooth Powder (B)

F. S. Cleaver's Cherry Tooth Paste (A)

F. S. Cleaver's Circassian Cream (A)

Cleveland's Walnut Pomade (B)

Cold Cream (A)

Common's Areca Nut Tooth Paste (A)

Cook's Tooth Soap (B)

W. T. Cooper's Carnation Tooth Paste (B)

Cork Chemical & Drug Co.'s Cold Cream of Roses (B)

Cornell & Cornell's Emolline (A)

Cousins, Thomas & Co.'s Rose Cold Cream (A)

Cracroft's Areca Nut Tooth Paste (A)

Cracroft's Cherry Tooth Paste (A)

Crosse & Blackwell's Anchovy Paste (A)

Crown Perfumery's Cherry Tooth Paste (B)

Cullwick's Skin Ointment (B)

Curtis' Pommade Nettoyer (B)

Darby's Fluid Meat (B)

William Darling's American Dentifrice (B)

J. M. Davis & Son's Otto of Rose Cold Cream (A)

Dean's Cherry Tooth Paste (A)

T. H. Deane's Lodene Tooth Powder (B)

Decker's Sulphur Scurf Pomade (B)

Delcroix & Co.'s Pomade (B)

Delicately Perfumed Cold Cream (A)

H. Dixon's Cold Cream (A)

Dodd's Areca Nut Tooth Paste (A)

Dodd's Cherry Tooth Paste (A)

Douglas – Perfumer (A)

Robt Douglas' Cosmetics (A)

Robt Douglas' Concentrated Egg Julep (B)

Jean Dupont's Cherry Tooth Paste (B)

Durbin's Areca Nut Tooth Paste (A)

Durbin's Cherry Tooth Paste (A)

B. K. Earnshaw's Cold Cream (A)

R. B. Ede's Shaving Cream (B)

English Chemists' Cold Cream (A)

Erasmic Shaving Cream (C)

Evans' Cherry Tooth Paste (A)

E. Castell Evans' Cold Cream (A)

Eye Ointment (A)

Eynon's Cold Cream (A)

Dr Field's Sapiridine (B)

Mrs E. Filce's Ointment (C)

Richard Finegan's Nutritive Cream (B)

Fortnum & Mason's Anchovy Paste (A)

Fortnum & Mason's Caviar (A)

Fortnum & Mason's Chicken and Ham (A)

Fortnum & Mason's Mushroom Savoury (C)

Fortnum & Mason's Potted Beef (A)

Fortnum & Mason's Potted Game (B)

Fragrant Shaving Cream (A)

Freke & Co.'s Otto of Rose Cold Cream (A)

J. Fuller's Cherry Tooth Paste (A)

Gabriel's Royal Dentifrice (B)

George Gardner's Bear's Grease (C)

J. Gardner's Cherry Tooth Paste (A)

R. A. Gardner's Cold Cream (A)

Gelle Freres' Creme de Savon Dulcifie (B)

Gelle Freres' Pomade a la Violette de Parme (C)

Genuine Bear's Grease (C)

Genuine Russian Bear's Grease as Imported (C)

George & Welch's Carbolic Tooth Paste (A)

Gethen's Oriental Tooth Paste (A)

H. Gilbertson's Areca Nut Tooth Paste (A

H. Gilbertson's Cherry Tooth Paste (A

H. Gilbertson's Shaving Cream (A

Gilson's Anchovy Paste (A

Gilson's Cream of Bloater (A

Gilson's Cream of Prawns (B

Giles' Cherry Tooth Paste (A

Glaisyer's Cold Cream (B

W. A. Goodall's Otto of Rose Cold Cream (A

Gosling's Cosmetics (A

John Gosnell's Cherry Blossom Cream (A

John Gosnell's Cold Cream (A

John Gosnell's Cold Cream of Roses (A

John Gosnell's Genuine Bear's Grease (C

S. F. Goss' Areca Nut Tooth Paste (A

S. F. Goss' Cherry Tooth Paste (A

S. F. Goss' Otto of Rose Cold Cream (A

Grattan's Odoriferous Cold Cream (B

Gray & Sons' Shaving Cream (B

S. F. Gredo's Creme Chrysis (C

Mrs Green's Wonderful Ointment (C

W. J. Green's Red Rose Tooth Paste (B

Grossmith & Son's Rose Cold Cream (A

Guerlain's Cream for Shaving (A

Mrs Ellen Hale's Heal-All Ointment (C

Hanbury's Cold Cream (A

R. Hancock-Ungrub's Red Ointment (C

Hanson's Antiseptic Tooth Paste (B

Hanson's Perfection Dentifrice (B)

John Hardy's Scurf Pomatum (B)

Harrod's Areca Nut Tooth Paste (A)

Harrod's Bloater Paste (A)

Harrod's Cherry Tooth Paste (A)

Harrod's Gorgona Anchovy Paste (A)

Harrod's Otto of Rose Cold Cream (A)

Harsant's Golden Cream for Chilblains (B)

Dr Hassall's Hair Restorer (C)

J. B. Hay & Co.'s Cold Cream a la Rose (B)

Hedges & Son's Cold Cream of Roses (B)

Hempstead & Co.'s Areca Nut and Cherry Tooth Paste (A)

Hempstead & Co.'s Cold Cream of Roses (A)

Heppell & Co.'s Otto of Rose Cold Cream (A)

J. Hick's Rose Cold Cream (A)

J. Hick's Queen's Otto of Rose Cold Cream (B)

Hill's Eucalyptus Tooth Paste (B)

Hilton's Cold Cream (A)

Hobson's Lakeland Blossoms Tooth Paste (B)

Hockin's Areca Nut Tooth Paste (A)

Hockin's Cherry Tooth Paste (A)

Hockin, Wilson & Co.'s Carbolic Tooth Paste (A)

Hockin, Wilson & Co.'s Cold Cream (A)

Hodgkinson, Preston & King's Royal Cherry Tooth Paste (B)

R. Hogg's Areca Nut Tooth Paste (A)

R. Hogg's Cherry Tooth Paste (A)

R. Hogg & Son's Cold Cream (A)

Holloway's Ointment (B)

Holmes & Co.'s Cold Cream (A)

Home & Colonial Stores' Areca Nut Tooth Paste (A)

Home & Colonial Stores' Cherry Tooth Paste (A)

Home & Colonial Stores' Rose Cold Cream (A)

R. Hovenden's Bear's Grease (C)

R. Hovenden's Shaving Soap (A)

R. Hovenden & Sons' Creme d'Amande (B)

R. Howden's Cold Cream (A)

R. Howden's Rose Cold Cream (A)

Humphrey's Fragrant Tooth Paste (B)

Icilma Creme (C)

Icilma Cold Cream (B)

Imperial Hotel's Hairdressing Department (B)

Irman's Stores' Areca Nut Tooth Paste (B)

G. W. Isaacs' Carbolic Tooth Powder (A)

Charles Jaschke's Shaving Cream (A)

Jewsbury & Brown's Oriental Tooth Paste (A)

Jordan's Carnation Tooth Paste (B)

Josephson's Australian Ointment (C)

G. Joseau – Pharmacier Francais (A)

Junior Army & Navy Stores' Cold Cream of Roses (A)

Junior Army & Navy Stores' Pure Cold Cream of Roses (A)

Keddie's Bloater Paste (A)

Keddie's Gorgona Anchovy Paste (A)

Keene & Ashwell's Dentifrice (B)

Kingston's (Valetta, Malta) Superior Cold Cream (C)

Knowles' Esauline (B)

Laurence's Areca Nut Tooth Paste (A)

R. C. Layng's Areca Nut Tooth Paste (A)

F. Lecomte's Cold Cream (A)

Leslie's White Carbolic Tooth Paste (A)

Letherby's Logwood Pomade (B)

Lewis' Skin Pomade (B)

Lewis & Burrow's Areca Nut Tooth Paste (A)

Lewis & Burrow's Cherry Tooth Paste (A)

Lewis & Burrow's Otto of Rose Cold Cream (A)

Lewis & Burrow's Rose Cold Cream (A)

Lip Salve (A)

Lockyer's Cherry Tooth Paste (A)

Gustav Lohse's Saporal Aromatische Zahn Pasta (B)

London Soap & Candle Co.'s Ambrosial Shaving Cream (B)

Lorimer's Areca Nut Tooth Paste (A)

Lorimer's Cherry Tooth Paste (A)

Lorimer's Cold Cream of Roses (A)

Lorimer's Tooth Paste (A)

Maison Dorin (A)

William Maskew's Cherry Tooth Paste (B)

S. Mason & Sons' Carbolic Tooth Paste (A)

Martindale's Salicfrice Tooth Paste (C)

Mathew's Otto of Rose Cold Cream (A)

J. J. Matthias' Cherry Tooth Paste (B)

Maw, Son & Sons' Ambrosial Shaving Cream (B

Maw, Son & Sons' Areca Nut Tooth Paste (A

Maw, Son & Sons' Aromatic Tooth Paste (B

Maw, Son & Sons' Camphorated Tooth Paste (B

Maw, Son & Sons' Cherry Tooth Paste (A

Maw, Son & Sons' Indian Betel Nut Tooth Paste (B

Maw, Son & Sons' Otto of Rose Cold Cream (A

Maw, Son & Sons' Rose Tooth Paste (A

Maw, Son & Sons' White Carbolic Tooth Paste (B

Maw, Son & Sons' White Cherry Tooth Paste (A

Maw, Son & Sons' White Rose Toilet Powder (B)

Maw, Son & Sons' White Rose Tooth Paste (A)

Maw, Son & Thompson's Ambrosial Shaving Cream (B)

Maw, Son & Thompson's Areca Nut Tooth Paste (A)

Maw, Son & Thompson's Aromatic Tooth Paste (B)

Maw, Son & Thompson's Cherry Tooth Paste (A)

Maw, Son & Thompson's Indian Betel Nut Tooth Paste (B)

Maw, Son & Thompson's Otto of Rose Cold Cream (A)

Maw, Son & Thompson's Rose Tooth Paste (A)

Maw, Son & Thompson's White Cherry Tooth Paste (A)

Maw, Son & Thompson's White Rose Tooth Paste (A)

May, Roberts & Co.'s Areca Nut Tooth Paste (B)

McMaster, Hodgson & Co.'s Cold Cream of Roses (B)

Meacher & Higgins' Cold Cream (A)

Miller & Co.'s Rose Lip Salve (B)

F. Millot's Bear's Grease (C)

Mitchell & Eden's Shaving Cream (A)

Moore's Cherry Tooth Paste (A)

Morel Bros, Corbett & Sons' Anchovy Paste (A)

Morel Bros, Corbett & Sons' Chicken and Ham (A)

C. B. Morse's Castor Oil Pomade (C)

J. Mortimer's Areca Nut Tooth Paste (A)

F. C. Moss-Millar's Areca Nut Tooth Paste (A)

Neve's Shurzine Antiseptic Tooth Paste (B)

Neve & Co.'s Cold Cream (A)

F. Newberry's Areca Nut Tooth Paste (A)

F. Newberry's Cherry Tooth Paste (A)

F. Newberry's Old Englyssche Tooth Paste (B)

F. Newberry & Son's Cherry Tooth Paste (A)

Newcastle-on-Tyne Co-op's Areca Nut Tooth Paste (A)

Newcastle-on-Tyne Co-op's Cherry Tooth Paste (A)

Norris' Patent Shaving Soap (A)

O. G. & Co.'s Areca Nut Tooth Paste (A)

O. G. / Co.'s Cherry Tooth Paste (A)

O. S. Tooth Block (B)

Okell's Mona Tooth Paste (C)

Otto of Rose Cold Cream (A)

Pain & Bayles' Rose Cold Cream (A)

Parke's Drug Stores' Areca Nut Tooth Paste (B)

Parke's Drug Stores' Cherry Tooth Paste (A)

Parke's Drug Stores' Cold Cream of Roses (A)

Parke's Drug Stores' Otto of Rose Cold Cream (A)

A. Parker's Otto of Rose (A)

R. H. Parker's Areca Nut Tooth Paste (A)

R. H. Parker's Otto of Rose Cold Cream (A)

Parton & Osborne's Connaught Tooth Paste (B)

Partridges's Tooth Powder (A)

Patey & Co.'s Cold Cream (A)

Patey & Co.'s Genuine Bear's Grease (C)

Patey & Co.'s Superior Cold Cream (A)

F. Perkin's Cherry Areca Tooth Paste (B)

Phillips' Areca Nut Tooth Paste (A)

Phillips' Carbolic Tooth Paste (A)

Phillips' Cherry Tooth Paste (A)

Dr Pierrepont's Astringent Dentifrice (B)

Ed. Pinaud's Cold Cream (A)

Ed. Pinaud's Veritable Graisse d'Ours (C)

Plumley's Areca Nut Cherry Tooth Paste (A)

Pond's Areca Nut Tooth Paste (A)

Pond's Cherry Tooth Paste (A)

Pond's Cold Cream (A)

Pond's White Areca Nut Tooth Paste (A)

Dr. Posteel's Cherry Tooth Paste (B)

Potted Anchovies (A)

Potted Beef (A)

Potted Game (A)

Potted Ham and Chicken (A)

Potted Prawns (A)

Potted Shrimps (A)

Napoleon Price & Co.'s Bear's Grease (C)

Napoleon Price & Co.'s Cherry Tooth Paste (A)

Napoleon Price & Co.'s Edelweiss Tooth Paste (C)

Napoleon Price & Co.'s Prince Albert Shaving Cream (B)

Price & Gosnell's Bear's Grease (C)

Prosser Roberts' Areca Nut Tooth Paste (B)

Prosser Roberts' Cherry Tooth Paste (B)

Putey & Co.'s Genuine Bear's Grease (C)

J. Pye's Cherry Tooth Paste (A)

H. C. Quelch's Gardenia Tooth Soap (C)

Read's Menthene Tooth Paste (B)

Reading Central Drug Stores' Otto of Rose Cold Cream (A)

Real Gorgona Anchovy Paste (A)

C. Ricola's Royal Ambrosial Shaving Cream (B)

Rimmel's Glycerine Cream (A)

Rimmel's Saponaceous Cream of Almonds Shaving Cream (C)

Roberts' Areca Nut Tooth Paste (A)

Roberts' Cherry Tooth Paste (A)

Roberts' Cold Cream (A)

Roberts' Coralline Tooth Paste (C)

Roberts' Glycerine Cold Cream (A)

C. E. Robinson's Cold Cream (A)

Rogers' Cold Cream (A)

Rowland's Odonto (A)

Rowland's Otto of Rose Cold Cream (A)

St Paul's Areca Nut Tooth Paste (B

St Paul's Carbolic Tooth Paste (B

St Paul's Cherry Tooth Paste (B

St Paul's Tooth Paste (B

St Paul's White Carbolic Tooth Paste (B

St Paul's White Cherry Tooth Paste (B

St Paul's White Rose Tooth Paste (B

Salmon's Corn Ointment (B

Sandringham's Areca Nut Tooth Paste (A

Sandringham's Cherry Tooth Paste (A

Sandringham's Cold Cream (A

Sandringham's Otto of Rose Cold Cream (A

J. Sanger & Co.'s Areca Nut Tooth Paste (A

J. Sanger & Co.'s Carbolic Tooth Paste (A

J. Sanger & Co.'s Cherry Tooth Paste (A

J. Sanger & Co.'s Rose Tooth Paste (B

J. Sanger & Co.'s White Rose Tooth Paste (A

Santin's Tooth Paste (A

Saunders' Areca Nut Tooth Paste (A

Saunders' Carbolic Tooth Paste (A

Saunders' Red Cherry Tooth Paste (B

Savar's Areca Nut Tooth Paste (A

Savar's Cherry Tooth Paste (A

Savoury & Moore's American Dentifrice (B

Savoury & Moore's Areca or Betel Nut Tooth Paste (A

Savoury & Moore's Cold Cream (A

Savoury & Moore's Cold Cream of Roses (A)

Searcy's Oriental Salt (B)

Searcy's Potted Meat (A)

Searcy, Tansley & Co.'s Oriental Salt (A)

Sharp Bros' Tooth Paste (A)

Sharp & Son's Cold Cream of Roses (A)

J. Shoolbred's Areca Nut Tooth Paste (B)

Skelton's Circassian Cream (A)

Squire's Cold Cream (A)

Squire's Tooth Paste (A)

R. S. Starkie's Rose Cold Cream (A)

Stennett & Coupland's Cold Cream (A)

Stone & Sons' Cherry Tooth Paste (A)

Sussex Co-op Drug Co.'s Rose Cold Cream (A)

Wm. Sutton & Co.'s Cherry Tooth Paste (A)

J. W. Taplin's Cold Cream (A)

Wm. Tapp's Shavaline (B)

G. H. Tatham's Shaving Cream (B)

Edward Taylor's Cherry Tooth Paste (A)

Edward Taylor's Cold Cream (A)

Edward Taylor's Imperial Tooth Paste (B)

Edward Taylor's Oriental Tooth Paste (A)

R. Thomas' Otto of Rose Cold Cream (A)

Thornton's Anthracoline Deodoriser (B)

Thornton's Toilet Cream (A)

Fred Tree's Cold Cream (A)

H. P. Truefitt – Perfumer (A)

H. P. Truefitt's Ambrosial Shaving Cream (B)

H. P. Truefitt's Egg Julep (B)

H. P. Truefitt's Genuine Bear's Grease (C)

Walter Truefitt's Almond Shaving Cream (B)

Walter Truefitt's Ambrosial Shaving Cream (B)

Walter Truefitt's Hair Cutting Rooms (B)

Universities Toilet Club's Saponaceous Cream of Almonds (B)

Viane's Shaving Cream (A)

Vinolia Shaving Soap (C)

Vinolia Tooth Paste (B)

Wand's Cherry Tooth Paste (A)

F. S. Weaver's Cherry Tooth Paste (B)

Weston's Cherry Tooth Paste (A)

Wesley's Petroleum Pomade (B)

Weston's Cold Cream (A)

Whitaker & Grossmith's White Cherry Tooth Paste (A)

Whitaker & Grossmith's White Rose Tooth Paste (A)

Charles White's Cold Cream (A)

Timothy White's Areca Nut Tooth Paste (A)

Timothy White's Cherry Tooth Paste (A)

Timothy White's Cold Cream (A)

Timothy White's Otto of Rose Cold Cream (A)

Whitehouse's No Name Ointment (A)

Mrs Williams' Nutritive Cream (B)

Williams & Elvey's Cold Cream (A)

Wilson's Areca Nut Cherry Tooth Paste (A)

Wilson's Rose Cold Cream (A)

Windle's Cherry Tooth Paste (A)

Windle's Cherry Areca Nut Tooth Paste (A)

A selection of pot lids recovered from Victorian and Edwardian refuse tips

The pot lids illustrated on the following pages have been arranged into three main categories: bear's grease, toothpaste, and cold creams and other beauty preparations.

The lids have been photographed actual size.

Bear's grease

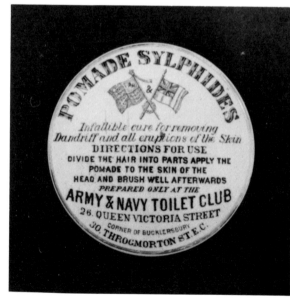

Toothpastes

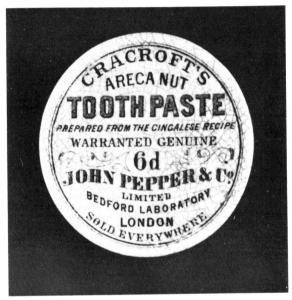

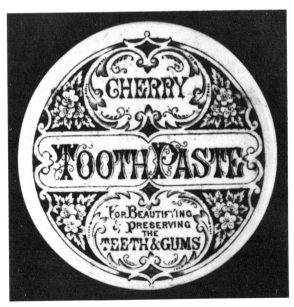

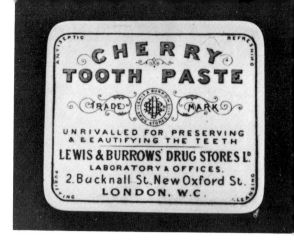

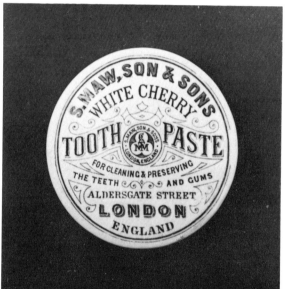

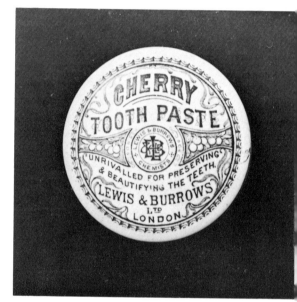

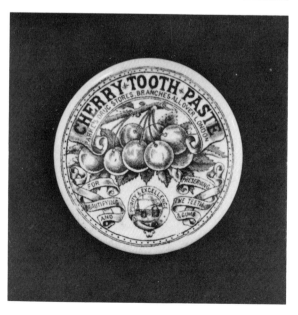

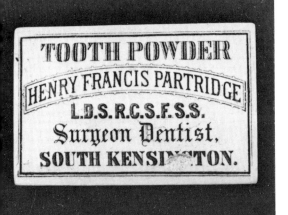

TOOTH POWDER
HENRY FRANCIS PARTRIDGE
L.D.S.R.C.S.F.S.S.
Surgeon Dentist,
SOUTH KENSINGTON.

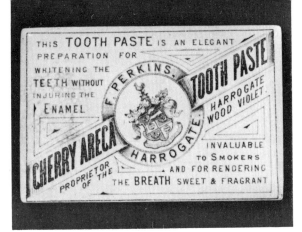

THIS TOOTH PASTE IS AN ELEGANT PREPARATION FOR WHITENING THE TEETH WITHOUT INJURING THE ENAMEL
F. PERKINS, HARROGATE
CHERRY ARECA
TOOTH PASTE
HARROGATE WOOD VIOLET
INVALUABLE TO SMOKERS AND FOR RENDERING THE BREATH SWEET & FRAGRANT
PROPRIETOR OF THE

CARBOLIC
TOOTH
PASTE

CALVERT'S CARBOLIC
TOOTH PASTE
TRADE MARK
SIXPENCE

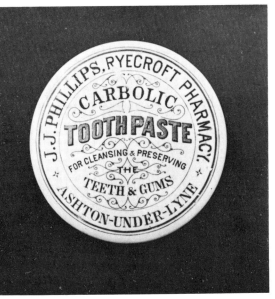

J.J. PHILLIPS, RYECROFT PHARMACY.
CARBOLIC
TOOTH PASTE
FOR CLEANSING & PRESERVING
THE
TEETH & GUMS
ASHTON-UNDER-LYNE

ARECA NUT TOOTH PASTE
BEAUTIFUL WHITE TEETH
MAY. ROBERTS & Cº LONDON

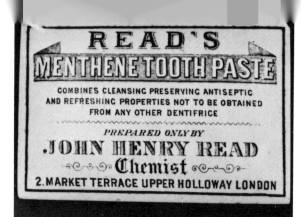

READ'S MENTHENE TOOTH PASTE

COMBINES CLEANSING PRESERVING ANTISEPTIC
AND REFRESHING PROPERTIES NOT TO BE OBTAINED
FROM ANY OTHER DENTIFRICE

PREPARED ONLY BY

JOHN HENRY READ

Chemist

2. MARKET TERRACE UPPER HOLLOWAY LONDON

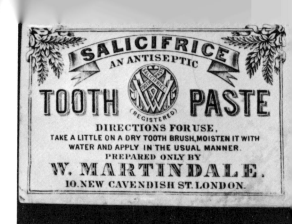

SALICIFRICE
AN ANTISEPTIC

TOOTH (REGISTERED) **PASTE**

DIRECTIONS FOR USE.
TAKE A LITTLE ON A DRY TOOTH BRUSH, MOISTEN IT WITH
WATER AND APPLY IN THE USUAL MANNER.
PREPARED ONLY BY

W. MARTINDALE.

10. NEW CAVENDISH ST. LONDON.

PREPARED BY
PEARLY WHITE
FOR THE
GUMS & TEETH
C. S. BENSTED DENTIST

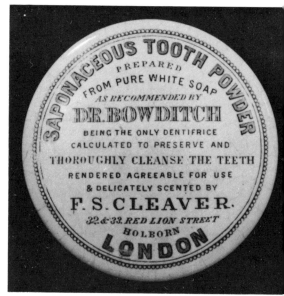

SAPONACEOUS TOOTH POWDER
PREPARED
FROM PURE WHITE SOAP
AS RECOMMENDED BY
DR. BOWDITCH
BEING THE ONLY DENTIFRICE
CALCULATED TO PRESERVE AND
THOROUGHLY CLEANSE THE TEETH
RENDERED AGREEABLE FOR USE
& DELICATELY SCENTED BY
F. S. CLEAVER.
32.&33. RED LION STREET
HOLBORN
LONDON

CHERRY
TOOTH PASTE
TRADE MARK
Co-operative
Wholesale Society Lᵈ
NEWCASTLE ON TYNE

MAW'S
INDIAN BETEL NUT OR ARECA
TOOTH PASTE
UNEQUALLED FOR   ITS SALUTARY
EFFECTS   ON THE
TEETH & GUMS
S. MAW. SON & THOMPSON
ALDERSGATE STREET
LONDON
ENGLAND

BURGOYNE, BURBIDGES' & Cos
FOR PRESERVING & BEAUTIFYING THE TEETH
TRADE MARK B.B & Co
CHERRY TOOTH PASTE

SAUNDER'S
RED CHERRY
AYTON & SAUNDERS TRADE MARK IXL
AYTON & SAUNDERS TRADE MARK IXL
TOOTH PASTE.
LIVERPOOL

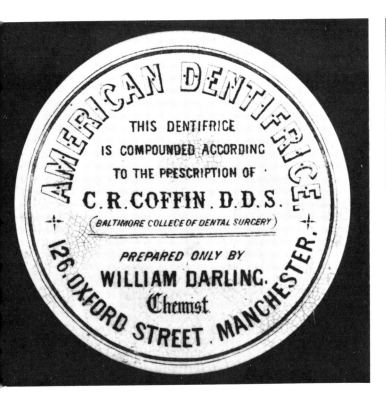

AMERICAN DENTIFRICE
THIS DENTIFRICE
IS COMPOUNDED ACCORDING
TO THE PRESCRIPTION OF
C. R. COFFIN. D.D.S.
(BALTIMORE COLLEGE OF DENTAL SURGERY)
PREPARED ONLY BY
WILLIAM DARLING.
Chemist
126, OXFORD STREET. MANCHESTER.

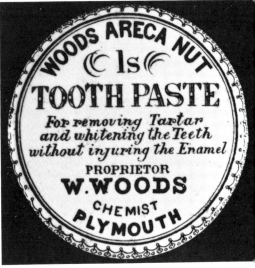

WOODS ARECA NUT
1s
TOOTH PASTE
For removing Tartar
and whitening the Teeth
without injuring the Enamel
PROPRIETOR
W. WOODS
CHEMIST
PLYMOUTH

99

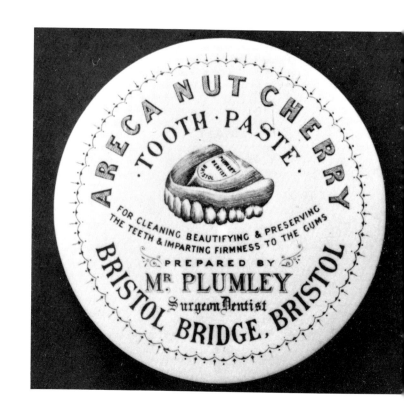

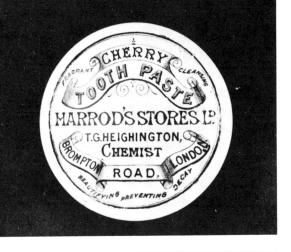

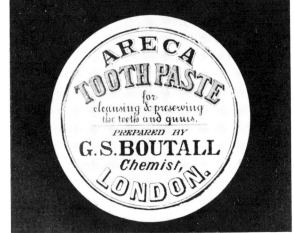

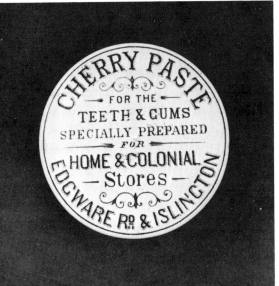

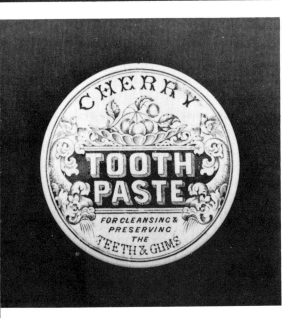

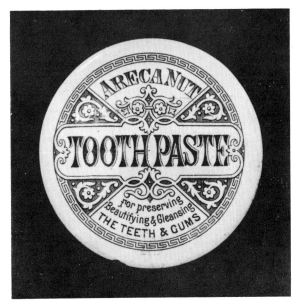

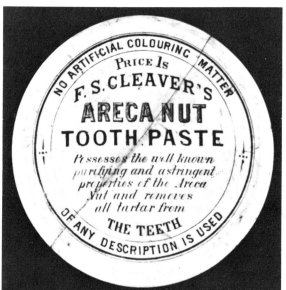

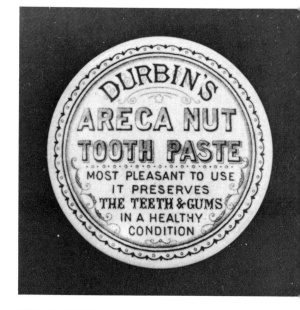

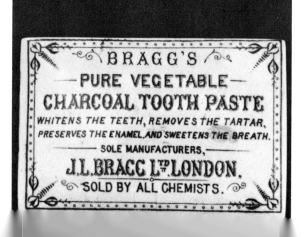

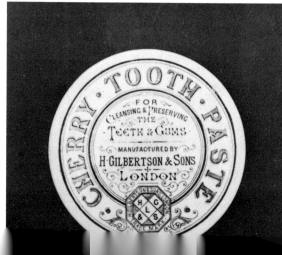

Cold creams and
other beauty preparations

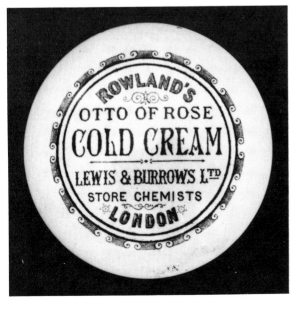

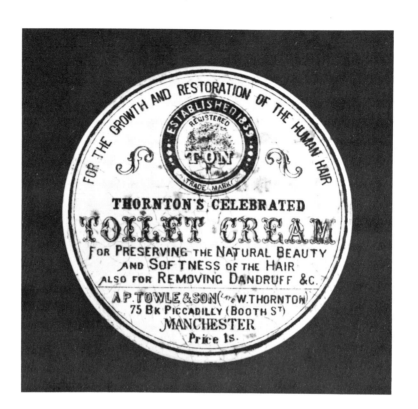

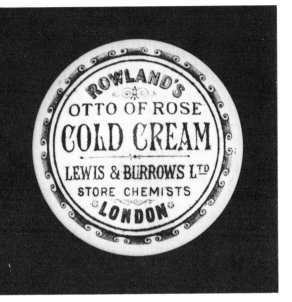

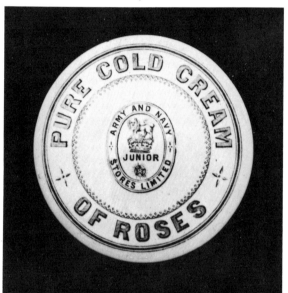

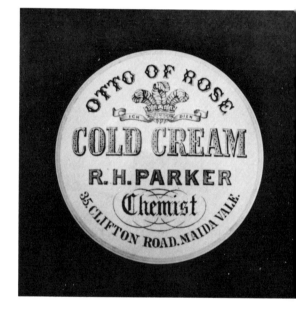

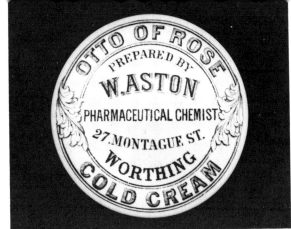

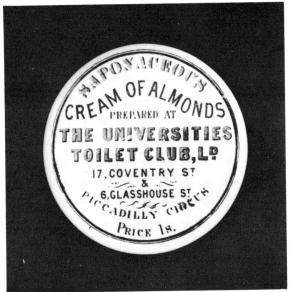

Others

Useful addresses, useful books

The British Bottle Collectors' Club
National Headquarters
'Greenacres'
Church Road
Black Notley
Braintree
Essex

Bottles and Relics News
9 Hambro Avenue
Rayleigh
Essex

Staffordshire Pot lids and their Potters, by C. Williams-Wood (Faber)

Bottle Collecting, by Edward Fletcher (Blandford Press)

Digging up Antiques, by Edward Fletcher (Pitman)

Index